An Introduction to Stillwater Fishing

An Introduction to Stillwater Fishing

David Batten

The Crowood Press

First published in 1990 by
The Crowood Press
Gipsy Lane, Swindon
Wiltshire SN2 6DQ

British Library Cataloguing in Publication Data

Batten, David
    An introduction to stillwater fishing.
    1. Great Britain. Still waters. Coarse fish. Angling
    I. Title
    799.11

    ISBN 1 85223 211 0

Typeset by PCS Typesetting, Frome, Somerset BA11 1EB.
Printed in Great Britain by Butler & Tanner Ltd, Frome.

Contents

Acknowledgements

Although any book is, of course, the author's own work, much of what he may write about is bound to have been influenced by contacts with others up to the point of putting pen to paper. It may not have been apparent at the particular moment in time that a contribution was made, but later when there is time to reflect we all recognise that we are influenced or guided by friends and contacts in all walks of life. With this in mind I would like to personally express my thanks to all those who have influenced my directions in angling and in the writing of this series of books.

Particular mention should be made of those who have directly helped with material, physical and psychological support during the many months spent researching, writing and illustrating, times when it seemed impossible that everything would come to fruition. My greatest thanks must go to my wife Kathy, who has had the task of preparing the manuscripts, indexes and turning out at all hours of the night to help obtain photographs for the book, and generally putting up with an angler who has not been able to go fishing as and when he wished!

My thanks go to Colin Brett, Chris Turnbull and John Wilson for their photographic contributions. Special mention is due to John who, in the midst of his own pressures of filming and writing, gave up precious time to take photographs for the cover of the book!

Thanks also to Mike Wood for his assistance in getting photographic material and references for the illustrations, and for his pleasant company on many successful and not so successful sessions!

Introduction

Every season many people take up angling for the first time whilst others return to it after a long lay-off following a major diversion in their lives, such as the pursuit of a career or getting married. In many cases the first tingle of interest comes through knowing somebody who catches a particularly big fish or reading about a notable capture in the local press. And many of these anglers are likely to start with some form of coarse fishing on a local stillwater.

Many newcomers today get started in angling by taking up carp fishing. Since most of the tackle and reading matter – not to mention baits – concentrates on this branch of the sport, this is not surprising. However, depending on success or failure, after a year or two many of these anglers begin to look for some new direction and inspiration, and this often leads to thoughts about all the other species there are to fish for. Few anglers have not accidentally caught quality roach, rudd, bream or tench, and even the occasional good perch which has taken a slowly retrieved brightly coloured boiled bait intended for carp. As the honeymoon period with carp fishing fades many begin to think seriously about giving the other species some deliberate attention with a view to catching them by design on the right balanced tackle which will provide greater enjoyment.

The better specimens which were easy to catch on carp baits and tackle will be rather harder to track down, attract and catch consistently on more suitable gear. For those who are at a take-off point in their angling career, and also for those who are thinking of starting stillwater fishing for the first time, the following pages will provide all the information required, through detailed illustrations and text based upon sound experience. If you are looking forward to the challenge of catching some of our more neglected species may I wish you every possible success and advise you to read on. I hope you enjoy what follows.

1 Fisheries

Today's anglers have access to a far greater variety of types of coarse fishery than have ever been available before. They include small farm ponds, estate lakes, gravel and clay pits, ornamental lakes and many other enclosed waters. Indeed, with care and planning any piece of water can easily be made into a coarse fishery.

Fisheries fall into perhaps three categories. The first is the club water, where club officials seek to offer a wide range of species for their members to catch. The second is the commercial fishery, which aims to offer good-quality fishing on a joint season- and day-ticket basis. Higher levels of different fish stocks are introduced to generate a wider interest in the sort of anglers who will pay for good-quality fishing. Some syndicate waters fall into this category as well, usually the type where good, high-quality fishing for several different species is available and where the growing on of large carp is secondary consideration and a bonus feature for the future. The third category is the carp syndicate water, the main reason for whose existence is to grow carp to the biggest possible size, to provide carp fishing of above-average quality for a small number of dedicated carp anglers. It is in this sort of fishery that you may find the odd exceptionally large fish of other species, since the need to control fish stocks by removal of unwanted species and smaller fish will always leave a few of each species to grow fat and fit on the abundant food supply that will be available.

All three categories have something to offer, but to varying degrees. The water owned or leased by a club, which may be heavily stocked to cater for the needs of club anglers, offers easy-to-catch fish. This is paramount in the success of the club, since poorly stocked waters result in poorly supported clubs. This fact sometimes overcomes club officials. It is presumed that the more fish, the greater the support for the club will be. This is certainly true but it can lead to heavy stocking of carp, which can be a mixed blessing. On the good side it provides easy fishing for club anglers and allows an easy introduction to carp fishing. The danger is that this type of water may quickly become uninteresting, leading members to seek new locations and fisheries.

Fish in well stocked or possibly overstocked waters may never reach the size everybody hopes they will. Because of lack of food and nutrients, competition for the amount of food available will be out of balance and the fish of all species will reach only the size their environment will allow, with some species being overrun and even wiped out by the pressure from a large species such as carp. If the water is a club fishery and perhaps the club's only water, heavy stocking with carp might actually be to the detriment of the club and many of its less intense members.

Is there a compromise to be made on fisheries? Very much so. Between these examples there *is* a fishery which will give satisfaction to everybody from the casual angler who would like to catch any of the species covered in this book, from rudd and roach through to

A small estate lake fishery, an ideal haunt for tench and the tench angler alike.

Low water levels in the summer of 1989 reveal many unknown features which may help location in the coming seasons.

The open aspect of a small gravel pit: note how the banks have been graded down to the water's edge to facilitate angling.

The open, almost ocean-like aspect of Weirwood Reservoir in Sussex.

A weed-choked and rubbish-strewn town-centre lake before being managed correctly for angling.

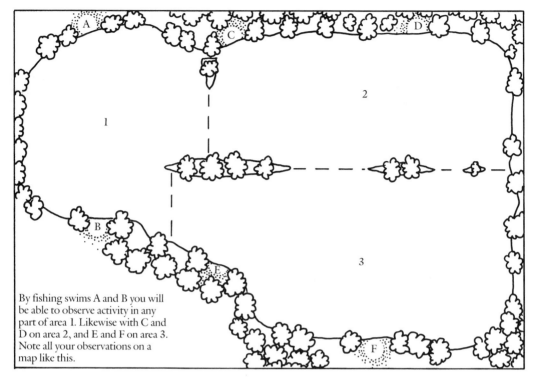

By fishing swims A and B you will be able to observe activity in any part of area 1. Likewise with C and D on area 2, and E and F on area 3. Note all your observations on a map like this.

Fig 1   Section fishing on larger lakes to observe fish activity.

the occasional carp, and on through the various levels of commitment up to the dedicated person who is a big-fish-only specialist angler.

What sort of fishery can cater for this sort of variety of style? The answer is a balanced and controlled fishery, where stocking levels and environmental conditions are monitored and controlled by fishery managers, owners and club officials. This means controlling the level of stocks of fish in order to gain maximum growth potential while at the same time maintaining the best health. The two go hand in hand, since only healthy fish grow, and healthy fish are more likely to survive a slight imbalance in their environment, which perhaps may be the result of adverse climatic conditions.

Controlling fish stocks may mean reducing the numbers of fish in order to maintain the best biomass levels, assessed by weight of fish per acre. For example, a reasonably rich water may support 1,000lb of fish per acre. This stock could be made up of 100 fish of 10lb each, or fifty fish of 20lb, or even 1,000 1lb fish per acre. Those weights and quantities might be distributed amongst several different species, such as roach, rudd, tench, carp and perch. It is important to have a mixture of species with different feeding requirements. Surface- and midwater-feeding species such as rudd and roach do not make heavy demands on the food reserves required by predominantly bottom-feeding species such as tench and carp.

With a balanced fishery you can cultivate a

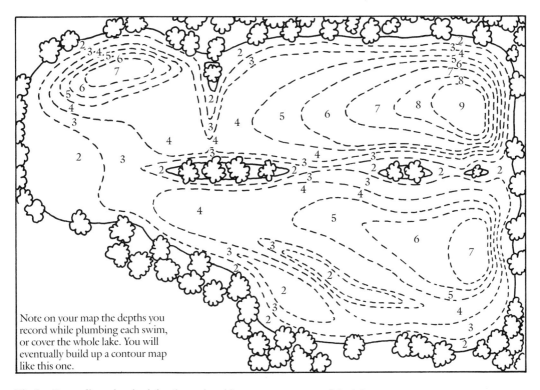

Note on your map the depths you record while plumbing each swim, or cover the whole lake. You will eventually build up a contour map like this one.

Fig 2   Recording plumbed depths and making a contour map of the lake.

water which will supply good fishing, with all the species mentioned growing to their optimum weight. If stocking levels are calculated slightly short of the maximum weight of fish per acre to allow for good growth, some fish will grow into their upper weight potential, giving the chance of a double-figure bream, a two-pound roach or a twenty-pound carp – maybe even more – and such a fishery will satisfy every kind of angler.

The whole question of stock levels, no matter what sort of size of fishery you look at, will decide how good or bad a fishery is. Too many fish in a small fishery can be as bad as too few in a large fishery.

What sort of fishery should you look for when getting started in stillwater fishing? After maximising the benefits of a balanced

fishery, my advice may seem rather perverse. Ideally you would be well advised to locate and investigate a well stocked fishery, perhaps an overstocked one if you can find one. Most areas of the country seem to have one commercially run fishery that will fit this bill.

The only way to learn anything about bait presentation and tactics is to catch fish regularly. If you can't catch on this sort of fishery you are doing something wrong and you certainly will not succeed on harder waters. Practice on an easy water teaches a lot about stillwater fishing.

The fishery to look for is one that is close enough for you to be able to fish it frequently and get to know it well. Learning how and when it fishes best, the times of day and weather conditions when it produces or does

Weed clearance and bankside rubbish collection and disposal begin in earnest.

not produce fish, is the first step to achieving the best results. Look for fishing related to your experience; learn to walk before you run. The weekly 'tackle for sale' columns are testimony to the many who fail by tackling the summit in their first season.

How do you find a good, well stocked fishery? Most good tackle dealers will be able to suggest a local day-ticket or club fishery which will give you the opportunity to catch a particular species. Fisheries vary from small, perhaps secluded manmade pools of, say, one or two acres to gravel pits of more than 200 acres. Similar features on different fisheries – shallow areas, deep areas, bars, snags, margins – will have similar characteristics, though differing in scale. Each area or feature will offer different problems to be overcome.

On completion of the management project, fish stocks are enhanced with the introduction of healthy new fish.

Good fishery management is about continual control of the fishery environment and balancing fish stocks. Netting of excess small fish allows checks on the quality fish at the same time.

Sunset over a Norfolk estate lake, and the swingtips wait motionless for the arrival of the angler's quarry, bream.

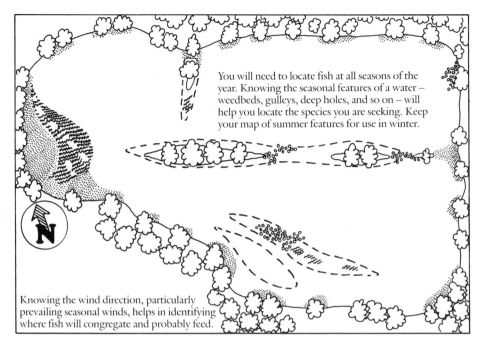

You will need to locate fish at all seasons of the year. Knowing the seasonal features of a water – weedbeds, gulleys, deep holes, and so on – will help you locate the species you are seeking. Keep your map of summer features for use in winter.

Knowing the wind direction, particularly prevailing seasonal winds, helps in identifying where fish will congregate and probably feed.

Fig 3   Features and wind directions on the lake.

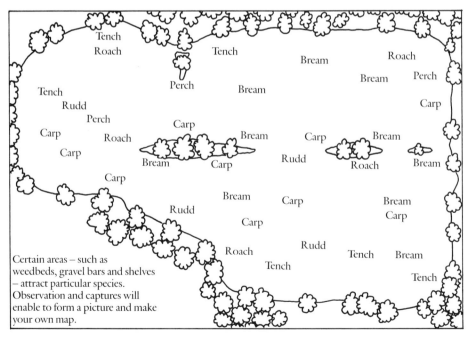

Tench
Roach
Tench
Bream
Roach
Bream
Perch
Tench
Rudd
Perch
Bream
Carp
Perch
Carp
Carp
Roach
Bream
Carp
Bream
Carp
Bream
Carp
Rudd
Roach
Bream
Roach
Bream
Carp
Carp
Bream
Carp
Bream
Rudd
Carp
Roach
Rudd
Roach
Tench
Bream
Tench
Tench

Certain areas – such as weedbeds, gravel bars and shelves – attract particular species. Observation and captures will enable to form a picture and make your own map.

Fig 4   Location of species – compare with contour and feature maps.

Observation of fish activity is easier on the smaller fisheries but the lessons learned can be usefully applied to fisheries of intermediate size and, indeed, to the largest waters.

The main thing to remember is *not* to jump around from fishery to fishery. Benefit first from the experience you gain. Once you have gained some sound experience, you can progress to the nearer big-fish waters and ultimately on to the more widely known big-fish waters throughout the United Kingdom and Europe.

2 Baits

When it comes to baits for fishing stillwaters your choice will to some degree be dictated by what you wish to catch. You may want to catch large quantities of smaller fish of all the listed species or you may want to seek out the bigger specimens. In either case you will find that successful anglers who share your preference will have favourite baits for particular species. Usually these are baits which have proved successful in regular use whilst others have failed to produce in identical situations. For the anglers concerned they have one important factor: they inspire confidence. With confidence in your bait you can concentrate on fishing better without being distracted by the niggling thought that the fish might not take your offering.

Some anglers become obsessed by a particular bait and instinctively use it for every species that may be in the lake, pit or pond. Whilst this may work, it can have the opposite effect and prevent the angler from catching as well as he might. Some baits do catch many species but at times a change in bait may give bigger rewards.

At the other extreme some anglers who fish either for specimens or quantities of fish chase and use all sorts of different baits without giving any one a serious trial. In many cases they carry a wide range of baits whenever and wherever they fish and for whatever species they may be targeting. Much of this is the result of reports in the angling press of a big catch or an especially big fish falling to a particular bait. Whilst a great deal can be learned from reports of others' successes,

much of what you read may have no bearing on the water you fish or intend to fish. One disadvantage of copying others is that you are presenting a bait that the fish have been educated about through repeated capture and which they will avoid. Witness the drop in captures to a particular bait in mid-July which saw fish after fish being caught on it in the opening days of the new season. This is education by association.

Each season sees the appearance of new 'super baits' which are guaranteed to catch particular species, perhaps a ready-to-use bait or perhaps an additive which will make the chosen bait attractive to a particular species. It is very easy to fall into the trap and buy all these specials, but you will eventually realise that the angler himself is the one most often caught. To be fair, some of the additives that come on the market each year do work and occasionally some are extremely successful. The disadvantage is that if they are successful then everybody else soon catches on to them as well. One good idea is to note their success and resume using them when everybody else is using something else. Remember education by association: fish soon learn to avoid popular baits – popular, that is with anglers, not just with fish. A few months or a new season will find the fish willing to take last year's super bait and with luck you may be the only angler who is using it this year and next.

To achieve your goal and to be consistently successful it pays to fish a different bait from everybody else, particularly in the middle of the season. Be observant, find out what is in use and vary your bait. A change of colour or flavour may be all that is necessary. But do not change too often; wait until there are definite signs that fish are not taking the bait any more and bites stop before you change.

Once the choice of bait has been made the next most important thing is its quality. There is no substitute for good-quality bait of any type, whether you intend it for lots of small fish or their specimen-sized brethren. We all come to witness the situation in which of two anglers fishing side by side and fishing identical methods and bait one catches all the fish. It is likely that the one who fails to catch has not chosen to clean his maggots or use a good-quality ingredient in his bait or groundbait. It takes very little effort to make sure that you are using a good clean attractive bait.

There is a real need to condition yourself into thinking about bait – its type, its condition and its quality. Once you do this, wherever and whenever you fish you can relax and concentrate on fish location and tackle presentation in order to enhance your catch rate. It is a matter of confidence: you will know instinctively that your chances of catching are good if you have made the effort with bait preparation.

Many of the species discussed in later chapters will take many of the following baits. Where specific recommendations are made for particular species that does not mean that only that bait will work. Experiment if you feel another bait might catch better. Some of the bigger species and specimens can be caught on the most basic baits, even on such humble offerings as bread flake.

BREAD BAITS

There are three basic bread baits – flake, crust and paste. Each has its own special require-ments in preparation and use. Bread flake is probably the most underused but most abused of baits. We may start to use it in the early days of our angling career, but few succeed in catching consistently with it. There are many problems that can defeat the flake angler. You may get the bites but fail to hook the fish, or you may find that you cannot keep the bait on the hook during the cast. It may be that you are using the wrong bread for flake. The best is undoubtedly a supermarket cut loaf. A good fresh-baked loaf is superb but they tend to vary in quality and can be very unreliable in staying workable for longish periods. A good fresh cut loaf will be moist and will require only a light pinch to set it on the hook. If it requires a hard pinch to get the flake to stay on the hook this usually means that there is a risk that it will not come off on the strike and may blind the hook from finding a hook hold when you strike. Figure 5 shows the correct way to attach flake – a firm pinch in the middle with plenty of fluffy flake round the edge. Remember, if it comes back on the hook during the retrieve it is not correctly mounted; it should always come off the hook very easily once it has been in the water for a few minutes. The only thing to vary is size of the piece of flake you use for each species – a smaller piece for rudd and roach and larger portions for tench, bream and carp.

While ideal for flake, the supermarket loaf is not suitable for crust. Here a fresh-baked loaf is preferable, and an ideal loaf is the sandwich loaf with its high soft crust content. Crust can be used for surface fishing or suspended off the bottom at variable depths for roach, rudd and carp. Figure 6 shows some methods of mounting and fishing bread crust. Pieces may vary from fingernail size for roach to matchbox size for carp, presented on the surface. Surface-fished crust can be given a different colour or even an added flavour.

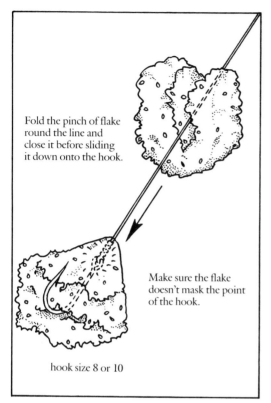

Fold the pinch of flake round the line and close it before sliding it down onto the hook.

Make sure the flake doesn't mask the point of the hook.

hook size 8 or 10

Fig 5   Bread flake on the hook.

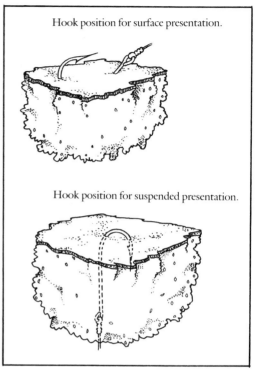

Hook position for surface presentation.

Hook position for suspended presentation.

Fig 6   Attaching crust.

Waterfowl do not spot coloured crust so easily and the addition of flavouring such as Marmite or peanut butter can enhance the bait's attraction for carp, which may be cautious about plain floating crust.

Adding ingredients to crust is not the only way of increasing the attractiveness of bread. You can add the same ingredients to your bread flake for bottom fishing or you can make up a bread-based soft paste bait.

When it comes to making paste either type of loaf can be used as there are two ways of mixing a bread paste. With both you will need to remove the crusts completely. With a sliced loaf lay out the number of slices you wish to use. Five or six will give a reasonable amount

of paste, but use more if you wish. Cover them liberally with the additive – liver pâté, honey, Marmite, fish paste, or whatever you fancy might attract your quarry. Stack the slices on top of one another and, over a large mixing bowl, squeeze the bread between your hands, squeezing and kneading the ingredients until you have a smooth paste of uniform texture. It may take as much as ten minutes, but every minute is worth it when you end up with a smooth lump-free soluble paste.

With a fresh uncut loaf, cut it into even slices and follow the same procedure. If you wish you can use stale bread and crumble the two ingredients together in a mixing bowl. You may need to add water to make it more workable, but if you use a moist additive this will be minimal. Probably the first method will suit you best, and it is so simple.

The size of the hookbait should be varied to suit the quarry species. A soft paste can sometimes work where hard baits fail, the fact that bread bait is soluble allows the flavour to leach out steadily, increasing the bait's attractiveness.

Plain bread paste can also be used. This is best made with stale bread and water, or perhaps milk. Bring it to a creamy consistency by adding crumbled bread until the texture is smooth and soft.

MAGGOTS

Maggots are available everywhere, are easy to use and will catch almost every species that swims in lake or river. The fact that all this is true leads to the misuse of maggots and a lot of disappointment. The humble maggot in one of its three forms – the large white, the pinkie and the squatt – is so readily available that many anglers pop into their nearest tackle dealer and purchase a half-pint or pint of whichever maggot is available (in many cases it will be plain white or a mix of white and coloured maggots) and proceed to go fishing the same day or the following day with what they presume is a good bait, without a thought about the condition, other than to comment that the bait smells badly.

Dealer Attitude

The maggot is an excellent bait, but the quality of a shop-bought supply depends on the dealer's attitude to his bait. If he has no interest in angling and the shop operates in some commodity as well as fishing tackle, it is unlikely that time will be available for bait care. The bait will be stored in a refrigerator in the same medium as it is supplied in by the

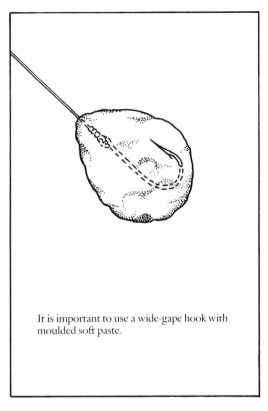

It is important to use a wide-gape hook with moulded soft paste.

Fig 7   Moulded paste on the hook.

maggot farm, invariably sawdust. This will become very smelly and contaminated, which will undoubtedly deter fish from taking the bait when it is offered on the hook. Some of the bait will also be old and may start to turn to casters within hours.

The Good Dealer

A good tackle dealer who sets out to give anglers a good service, both in tackle and bait, will take the trouble to set up a proper system of bait care. This will start with cleaning off the sawdust in which the maggots are supplied, using a vibrating riddle. The cleaned maggots will then be placed in clean

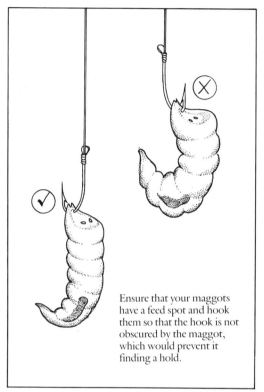

Ensure that your maggots have a feed spot and hook them so that the hook is not obscured by the maggot, which would prevent it finding a hold.

Fig 8   Hooking maggots.

Fig 9   Riddling maggots.

trays and ground maize added to further clean and freshen them. They are then refrigerated until sold. While the storage continues, intermittent turning and riddling goes on to remove any dead maggots, skins or casters. At the point of sale the bait will again be topped up with ground maize to keep it clean and fresh.

Match Anglers

Clearly the latter is the dealer to patronise if at all possible. Match anglers will usually frequent the better dealer so ask where they get their maggots. If you cannot find such a dealer then you will have to make do with the 'dirty' local supply and take steps to get the bait up

to the necessary standard. The need for this is unquestionable. If you really wish to be successful at catching fish of any species, the bait must be of the highest possible quality.

If you opt for using the local supply, be it dirty, moderate or first-class, there is one practice which will improve them all. If you have to buy your maggots from the local corner shop, it is worth finding how many gallons of maggots are used weekly and how often the dealer gets fresh supplies. If you can find a shop that gets a weekly supply, find out on which day the bait arrives and buy your bait as soon after as possible. A good fresh maggot has a black feed spot which is visible through the skin. Maggots without it may be quite old.

Clean and Prepare Your Own

If you have fresh maggots, when you arrive home riddle them clean of the sawdust or whatever they are supplied in with a riddle tray by shaking the tray briskly over a large container. Recover any maggots that drop through and then tip the maggots into a bowl containing ground maize or dampened bran and allow them half an hour to wriggle and clean themselves. Repeat the process, put the maggots into fresh dry bran and then place them in the refrigerator to keep them cool. It is important not to put too many maggots into a bait box; if in doubt use two boxes. The bait needs room to breathe; squashing too many maggots into a box makes them sweat and become smelly. Even with the better bait supply a change from the original maize to fresh maize or bran will help keep the bait in top condition. Make a habit of cleaning your bait when you buy it and you will gain an edge in catching more fish.

A good selection of clean, fresh maggots in the four most popular colours.

Coloured Bait

Coloured maggots, in whichever colour you wish, are best purchased ready-dyed. The professional colouring is stronger and costs no more anyway. Red, bronze and pink are the most popular colours after white. Colours are considered in more detail in later chapters.

CASTERS

For many species casters can prove a superior bait, but they have to be just right. Like maggots, if the bait is not at its peak of attraction and quality it will be rejected. For many years the caster was discarded as useless by many anglers who used maggots. However, on days when a high percentage of maggots turned to caster just before and during fish-

Loading a Drennan feeder link with maggots before fitting back the top cap.

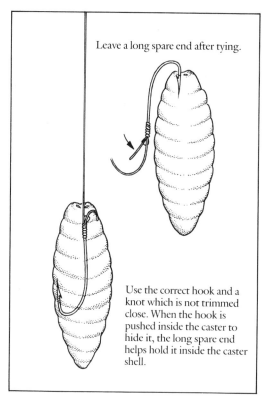

Leave a long spare end after tying.

Use the correct hook and a knot which is not trimmed close. When the hook is pushed inside the caster to hide it, the long spare end helps hold it inside the caster shell.

Fig 10   Hooking casters.

ing, the casters in the loose feed had the effect of conditioning the fish to feed on casters instead of maggots. Fish would be seen feeding but not taking hookbaits. It was then discovered that at certain stages in the casters' development they sank. If the supply of casters is in this condition feeding with loose caster and hooking single caster carefully can produce bumper bags as the fish, of all species, become preoccupied with a delicious bait.

Top-quality casters can be obtained from *good* tackle dealers. To produce good-quality casters requires the continuous care and interest of the dealer, who must riddle them off several times a day to ensure that they are collected and stored in peak condition. This is often too much for many tackle shops, but the ability to supply good-quality casters ensures that the tackle dealer gains good trade from regular customers, so it will pay to locate a good source and use it regularly.

Home-Produced Casters

It is possible to produce casters at home; we all do it to some degree. The difficulty is producing the quantity we may need at exactly the right moment. If you wish to produce your own casters make sure you buy fresh maggots with the feed spot visible, which will ensure that the bait is fresh from the bait breeder. Make sure that you have bait of one age. Some dealers supply bait of mixed supplies, which will mean casters being produced over several days instead of within several hours.

Quality Casters

The secret of turning casters is to allow them space and air to breathe and to keep turning them to ensure that they all get exposed to the warmth of the environment. The warmer the place of storage the quicker the caster will turn, but do not be tempted to speed this up by using excessive heat. Equally, the cooler it is the slower the turning will be. If you have taken into consideration the age of your maggot supply, you will get a fairly even turn from maggot to caster. If this is so, all you need do is periodically riddle the maggots that are still alive through a proper mesh riddle tray (Figure 9). As the casters are obtained they should be placed in polythene bags. Expel the air by gentle squeezing and tie the bags tight to keep it out. The bagged casters can be kept in the refrigerator. Good casters will be a golden bronze colour but any caster lighter in colour will be ideal for storage. The dark-ruby-coloured ones are usually no good because they will float. Check by dropping them in water if you are unsure.

HEMPSEED

Powerful Attractor

Whilst it makes an excellent hookbait, the real use for hempseed with most anglers today is as an attractor. This may be loose feed placed into the swim by hand, catapult, or swim feeder. Hempseed has the effect of attracting by sight and smell and will usually draw and hold fish in a swim, allowing an alternative hookbait to be offered directly among the bed of hemp. An example of this is the use of sweetcorn or boiled baits fished over hemp for roach, tench and carp. The hemp acts as the attractor, preoccupying the fish, which then takes the alternatively baited hook.

Natural Oils

There is a theory that hempseed, when properly cooked, resembles a snail and when presented in large quantities it resembles a natural bed of snails. Whether this is true or not will be for you to ponder. One thing is for sure – the sight of the white inner flesh of the cooked and split hempseed is very attractive visually. However, it is just as likely that the attraction comes from the natural oil released from the cooked hemp. Certainly the first attractive feature for the fish is likely to be the smell, with the small white tail perhaps aiding visually.

Cooking Hemp

Preparing hempseed is very simple. Presoaking for a few hours is beneficial but the seed can be cooked straight from the bag. Place a pint of it into two pints of water in a saucepan, bring it to the boil and then leave it to simmer for as long as it takes to open the shell of the seed and release the white inner flesh – approximately 15–20 minutes. Once this is

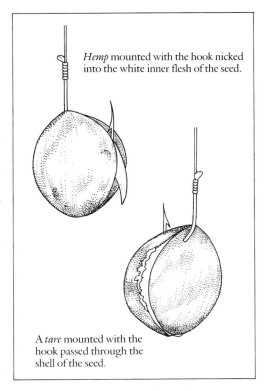

Hemp mounted with the hook nicked into the white inner flesh of the seed.

A *tare* mounted with the hook passed through the shell of the seed.

Fig 11   Hemp and tares on the hook.

complete the hempseed is ready for use either as an attractor or as a hookbait. Allow the bait to cool in its own juices and retain the liquid for use in ground bait or as a liquid attractor which can be poured into the swim at intervals to increase the attractor levels. An alternative is to freeze the liquid into blocks in an ice-cube tray and attach them to a leger weight with a piece of thread frozen into the blocks, or freeze a stone in the cube to make them sink quickly.

Flask-Cooked Hemp

The second way of preparing hemp is to put about a pint in a large two-pint vacuum flask and pour on boiling water, leaving a small space at the top. Replace the cap and leave for

6–8 hours, usually overnight. When you open the flask the hempseed should be suitably cooked and ready for use.

Ground Hemp

Ground uncooked hempseed can be a useful ingredient in a groundbait mix. The natural oils are released along with the ground seed, generating a high level of attraction. The addition of this form of hempseed to your own mix could prove very rewarding.

Hemp on the Hook

The art of using hempseed as hookbait is to mount it either on the hook as a single grain

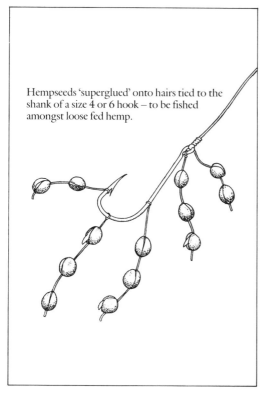

Hempseeds 'superglued' onto hairs tied to the shank of a size 4 or 6 hook – to be fished amongst loose fed hemp.

Fig 12   Hemp on hairs.

or as a multiple-grain presentation on a hair or hairs. The various methods can be seen in Figures 11 and 12. Which method you use depends on which species you are after. Single grains are ideal for roach with a fine-wire hook of suitable size, 16 or 18, whilst multiple baits on hairs are suitable for larger species such as tench or carp!

TARES

The minute size of hempseed makes hooking tedious. There are alternatives. One is to use one of the commercially made imitation hempseeds which you never need to change or rebait. The second is to use tares for hook-baits instead. The tares are slightly larger and are softer in texture once cooked, which makes presentation and hooking far better.

Preparing Tares

Tares are prepared in much the same way as hempseed, with the exception that the addition of a pinch of bicarbonate of soda will help them retain the black colour normally lost during cooking. Add two pints of water to a pint of tares and leave them to soak, ideally overnight. There is less in the way of natural attractor in the form of oil in tares so it could prove useful to add your own after cooking. The liquid flavours used in carp baits can be used with a great effect. Hempseed and maple flavourings are ideal.

Cooking Tares

Once soaked, place the tares in a saucepan, bring to the boil and then leave them to simmer for 15–20 minutes. After 10 minutes check the bait regularly until it is *just* cooked. Cooking in a vacuum flask works reasonably well but the saucepan is more efficient. Allow the bait to cool in its own juice and drain when cold.

WORMS

The only really good worm is a lively one, though half and tail sections do catch fish. Lobworms, redworms, brandlings and the rest make a handy bait when trying to tempt wary feeding fish which may be seen at close range. They are also useful when fish are feeding in silty areas. Even if the worm is out of sight the vibration of its wriggling will be felt by the probing sensitive barbels on most cyprinids snouts. Figure 13 shows how to attach worms to the hook and Figure 44 shows their presentation. Where would you use worms? A supply of worms is worth having if you are fishing small waters where the fish can be seen feeding close in, present the worm or worms on lightly weighted float tackle for exciting sport.

SWEETCORN

If any particular bait took angling into a new phase it was sweetcorn. It is cheap, readily available everywhere and is easily stored and carried. More important, it attracts and catches just about every stillwater species you will find in your waters. Even pike are caught on it when tackle is being retrieved, the bright-yellow grains attracting a close-lying pike to strike as they spin by.

This bright-yellow colouring, which makes the bait easy to find by sight, is most definitely part of the attraction. Add to this the attractive natural flavour and you have a bait that is not often refused. At times, however, bites on ordinary sweetcorn become difficult to hook and eventually virtually cease. It is most likely that, once many fish have been caught on

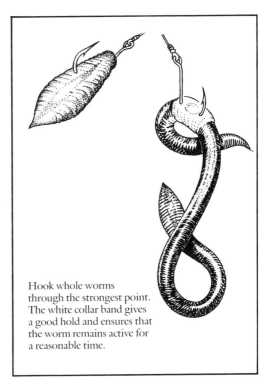

Hook whole worms through the strongest point. The white collar band gives a good hold and ensures that the worm remains active for a reasonable time.

Fig 13   Lobworms on the hook.

sweetcorn in the early season, the bright colouring and the flavour help the fish associate the bait with danger. This may occur during late July or early August and twitches on the float or indicator may be the only sign you will get of bites.

When this happens, changing the colour of the sweetcorn, or its flavour, or both, can restore its attraction. Slowly adding small quantities of red or brown bait colourings to the corn until the right colour is achieved will make it less obvious; and the addition of 5 millilitres of strawberry or caramel flavouring, or any one of the many carp bait flavours available, plus 5 millilitres of concentrated sweetener will change the flavour enough to fool the fish into taking the bait again. Bear this in mind when you are using corn; change to an alternative before everyone else does and catch a few more fish.

PARTICLE BAITS

How do you fish with sweetcorn? Sweetcorn is a particle bait, many other baits fall into the same category and all are fished in similar fashion. Particles are any small bait which is fished in quantity and include peas, beans, nuts, seeds and any large bait such as boiled baits diced or rolled to a small size.

There are many different varieties, too many to list every one. Some of the most successful are maple peas, chick peas, black-eye beans, peanuts and tiger nuts. All are dry in their original state and, unlike sweetcorn, require soaking and cooking prior to use. Some large supermarkets stock tinned varieties of particles such as red kidney beans, chick peas, cannollini beans, and the like, which offer a handy alternative. Their disadvantage is that they are usually cooked to a very soft state, which makes hooking a little difficult.

Since all the particle baits (see Appendix 1) are stored dry they will absorb water and subsequently swell to at least twice the dried size. To allow for this, when preparing any of them, including peanuts and tiger nuts, add twice as much water to the container as bait – for example, 2 pints of water with 2 millilitres of salt to 1 pint of bait. Soak for at least twenty-four hours, adding the water as necessary to keep the bait covered fully. If you intend to flavour your bait, it is best to add the flavouring to the water at the beginning of the soak. With 1 pint of bait add 10 millilitres of flavouring and perhaps 10 millilitres of sweetener if you use a sweet flavour, or increase the salt to 5 millilitres with a savoury flavour. Once soaking is complete you should place the bait and flavoured water in a saucepan or pressure cooker and cook until the bait is soft enough for hooking. Note how long this takes for future reference.

Cooking has the additional effect of neutralising harmful chemicals in some of the pea and bean varieties, notably red kidney beans. With the nuts, cooking breaks down and releases the natural oils in the nut, making for a natural attractor in conjunction with any added flavourings. With nuts it can be useful to add salt or sweetener to match the type of flavouring, and with all these baits it can pay to try a sweet-savoury mixture, particularly if everyone else is sticking to tradition!

SPECIAL BAITS

Some special baits are particularly useful if you wish to seek out some of the larger specimens of tench and carp. Many of the recipes used for these species are attractive to other species too and this is worth remembering when fishing gets slow on conventional baits.

These baits can be used either as soft paste baits or as boiled baits to avoid the attentions of smaller fish nibbling them away! The attraction is at its highest in the soft paste form, since the bait slowly dissolves, releasing into the water both the added flavour and any natural ones.

Most good tackle dealers today stock ready-made boiled baits and ready-mixed base mixes, to which you have only to add water to make paste baits or eggs to make boiled baits. They are listed in Appendix 1. You can also buy the necessary ingredients and mix your own. You will need to add flavouring, sweeteners and colourings to make the bait just as you wish. Remember the sweetcorn! For a 10oz mix 5 millilitres of flavouring and sweetener are all that is necessary, but refer to the suppliers' labels for their own suggested levels.

Method

Mix the ingredients thoroughly with either water or eggs. Always add the flavouring, sweetener and colouring to the liquids *before* you add the dry ingredients. Mix thoroughly, folding and kneading the bait until it is of an even texture. With soft pastes the bait must be left to stand to establish how firm a paste it is. Some ingredients take up a lot of water slowly and can become dry and crumbly. If the mix stays moist and may be too soft, add a little more dry mix until you get the required consistency. For boiled baits, use enough eggs to mix the bait, between three and six for a 10oz mix. Once mixed, roll it out into sausages, cut and roll them into baits of approximately ½ inch in diameter and drop them into a saucepan of boiling water for between 30 seconds and 2 minutes, depending how hard you wish to make your baits. A flour sieve is of great help when boiling a lot of baits at a time. Put the baits in it before immersing them in the boiling water.

If you choose to use ready-made boiled baits, makes such as Stream Select, Crafty Catcher and Rod Hutchinson's Catchum baits are superb fish catchers in many of their flavours. The choice is yours. Carp baits are discussed in greater detail in *An Introduction to Carp Fishing* in this series of books.

GROUNDBAITS

The choice of groundbaits is a matter for each individual angler's preference. Walk into any good tackle dealer's and you will see a large variety of good-quality groundbait mixes from one of the reputable manufacturers – British Ground Baits, Sensas and Marcel Van Den Eynde, to list a few. Some are listed in Appendix 1. Many of these are well proven mixes aimed at particular types of fisheries, as well as specific fish. Many are based on successful continental recipes using herbs, hemp and many other special ingredients for attraction, binding and other qualities.

Additives

The purpose of groundbaits and groundbaiting is to draw and hold your target species. Additives and specialised mixes will to some degree be necessary at some point, but it is very easy to get tied up in bait mixes and forget the fish. Understanding the practicalities of mixing and using groundbait is more important than getting deeply involved in the contents of groundbait mixtures. Groundbait contents should, to some degree, complement the hookbait. For example, when you use bread flake the ideal groundbait is mashed bread.

Mashed Bread

Mashed bread is simplicity itself since all you need is a small supply of stale bread. A sliced loaf left open for a couple of days will fit the bill. At the waterside, simply soak the bread in a bowl or in the mesh of the landing net and pour off or squeeze out the excess water. The resulting mushy, loose mix can be introduced into the swim in small quantities for prebaiting and groundbaiting.

Breadcrumb

Among the ready-prepared baits the most used is probably breadcrumb, which can be bought in packs from 1 to 25kg in white, brown or golden forms. On their own breadcrumbs constitute a basic feed for loose feeding and for swimfeeder plugging. With the basic breadcrumbs we will stop. Many additives can be used with them, including proprietary mixes from home and Continental suppliers.

Mixing Groundbait

The secret of which groundbait recipes will best suit a particular fishery can be learnt only through experimentation. More important than specific mixes is how to mix the groundbait to suit the circumstances on the fishery.

Texture

Many factors combine in the successful use of groundbait. You must have a good idea of the quantity of fish you are fishing amongst. Too much groundbait will not only draw and hold the fish but also overfeed them, which makes them less likely to take a hookbait. If the mix is too stiff it may lie on the bottom in a firm ball for too long and not actually attract any fish. If it is too loose and dry, it may break up on entry and attract a surface-feeding species such as rudd or a midwater-feeding species such as roach. This is fine if these are your quarry but of little use if you are after tench or bream – unless you are trying to introduce feed over their heads when they are known to be feeding.

The same occurs with the use of bread-crumb to plug open-end feeders and cage feeders: too firm a mix and the feeder will not release the bait samples; too loose and the bait will break up on hitting the water, again drawing the fish away.

General Attractor

The best groundbait will answer the circumstances. A bottom bait should not break up until it sits on the bottom, and should then break up slowly and draw the fish into the baited swim. A general attractor – a cloud-type bait – should break up progressively as it falls through the water, offering a wide band of small bait particles over a wide area.

Quantity

Consider carefully whether your groundbait is mixed to suit the swim and the fishing method. Is it of the right quantity to suit the fish population, attracting without overfeeding? Experiment to get the right results. Once you understand the basics, experiment with additives to add to the attraction. But do not forget the ground rules. Your early mixes should only carry the free hookbait samples in small quantities to encourage interest in the hookbait.

3 Tackle

The subject of tackle for stillwater fishing is a very large one and how you approach it will depend on just what you want to gain from fishing lakes, ponds, gravel pits, meres and reservoirs. So many anglers today seem to start with the wrong tackle. Perhaps tackle is bought as a present by a well intentioned non-angler. Perhaps a tight budget results in a choice of less than suitable tackle.

Whilst some tackle is suitable for various fishing techniques and quarry species there is little sense in taking the view that one rod and reel will be suitable for all the types of fishing you will wish to do. You can certainly get by in the early days catching small fish with a general-purpose float rod, but if you wish to become proficient at catching consistently then give the suggestions here some thought. Of course, if you only want to catch plenty of small fish a set of tackle chosen from the various items listed below will allow you to do just that. It is highly unlikely, however, that you will persist in that view for long. Many anglers move on after seeing the capture of some of the bigger species and you probably will too, so choose your tackle wisely.

RODS

Talk to any good angler and you will find that he has a rod to recommend for any given situation. His opinion will be based on his own success with the rod, possibly over a long period of time. Many of the rods recommended would once have been made of fibre-glass; today many are made of carbon fibre. More recently, new fibres have been incorporated with the carbon to improve the action and capabilities of the new rods.

The most successful new fibre in use has surely been Kevlar, and more recently Dyneemar from North Western. The new carbon-Kevlar mixture offers extreme strength, both in the rods' action in use and in general handling. Some of the more basic carbon rods costing about £20–30 suffer a serious shortcoming: the blanks contain very little carbon fibre and strength is accordingly reduced. An expensive fibreglass rod might well prove a better buy than a cheap carbon rod. Listed below are some recommended rods and blanks which will give you good service. The more you can afford to spend the better your investment will be, giving you the possibility of buying a lifelong tool that will serve you well.

In stillwater fishing you may be fishing many different types and sizes of water, from a small 1-acre pond to a 1,000-acre reservoir. Each of these waters and those in between will place varying demands on your tackle. You might be fishing a few yards from the bank in 3 or 4 feet of water or at ranges of over 100 yards in 30 feet of water – or anywhere in between. To get the full rewards from fishing in all of these situations you will need different rods.

For shorter-range fishing, either on the float or on the leger, a float rod of about 12–13 feet or a leger rod 11–12 feet will be necessary. It is easy to buy either. But when you

Make and Model	Material	Length	Features
Drennan Light Feeder	Carbon	11ft	2 tips ¾ and 1½oz
Drennan Medium Feeder	Carbon	11½ft	2 tips 1½ and 4oz
Drennan Heavy Feeder	Carbon	12ft	2 tips 2 and 4oz
Daiwa WK11TQTF Quivertip	Carbon/kevlar	11ft	2 tips (light, medium
Daiwa JCL10QT Quivertip	Carbon	10ft	3 tips and heavy)
Ryobi John Wilson Quivertip, AV110C	Carbon	11ft	2 top sections (quiver and Avon float), cork handle
Daiwa JCL 9½	Carbon	9½ft	Swingtip
Daiwa Harrier CWM13F	Carbon	13ft	
Daiwa Vulcan VCM13F	Carbon	13ft	
Drennan Specialist	Carbon	12ft	Lines 3–7lb BS
Drennan Waggler	Carbon	13ft	Lines 2–4lb BS
Drennan Tench	Carbon	13ft	Lines 5–8lb BS

Table 1   Recommended rods – the top eight are leger rods and the bottom five are float rods.

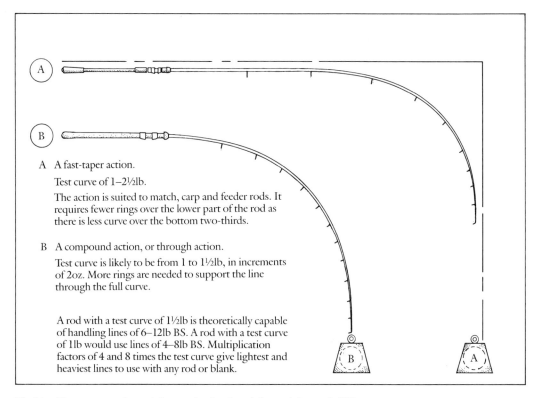

A   A fast-taper action.

Test curve of 1–2½lb.

The action is suited to match, carp and feeder rods. It requires fewer rings over the lower part of the rod as there is less curve over the bottom two-thirds.

B   A compound action, or through action.

Test curve is likely to be from 1 to 1½lb, in increments of 2oz. More rings are needed to support the line through the full curve.

A rod with a test curve of 1½lb is theoretically capable of handling lines of 6–12lb BS. A rod with a test curve of 1lb would use lines of 4–8lb BS. Multiplication factors of 4 and 8 times the test curve give lightest and heaviest lines to use with any rod or blank.

Fig 14   Test curves – the weight required to bend the rod through 90°.

consider what species you will be fishing for, what lines you will use, and so on, all of a sudden it is not so easy.

Float and leger fishing at close or medium range, up to 30 yards, will require rods with a medium action and a minimum length of 12 feet for the float rod and 11 feet for the leger rod, though 12 feet is more practical here as well. The float rod should be able to handle lines up to 4 or 5lb and the leger rod should handle lines of 5–6lb BS. Both the rods should be of medium to through action to allow bigger species to be controlled safely. Stiff, tip-actioned rods can risk line breakage or hooks being torn out on the strike at close range.

A range of more than 30 yards really calls for leger fishing, though some heavy float fishing can be done up to 50 yards. Rods for both are identical. At this sort of range you will be likely to use either straight leger weights or swimfeeders to carry out the bait and quantities of free feed and groundbait up to 60 or 70 yards. The demands on the rod are twofold: it must be capable of casting up to 2oz of loaded swimfeeder and of the hooking and playing a fish at this range. This will require a purpose-designed rod of a medium to tip action. A through-actioned rod could be used at the shorter range but hooking capability will be reduced.

The term 'test curve' comes into use with rods of the type discussed here. To meet the demands of this sort of fishing you will require a rod with a test curve between 1¼ and 1¾lb. Such a rod will handle lines of between 5 and 8lb BS, which are necessary to withstand the forces of casting heavy loaded swimfeeders.

For the heavier species of fish such as carp and tench, rods of heavier action and test curve will be necessary both for close-range work and distance casting and hooking. These are likely to have test curves from 1½ to

2½lb and handle lines from 9 to 15lb BS for casting up to 3oz of lead and bait. These rods will be much thicker in the wall than the rods mentioned above in order to withstand the pressure of compression on casting. The ideal length is 12 feet.

Specific recommendations as to rod type and action are given for the various quarries and fishing methods in the chapters that follow.

REELS

As with rods, there has also been a revolution in reel design. The most noticeable improvement is the reduction in weight of many reels to just a few ounces. This results from the

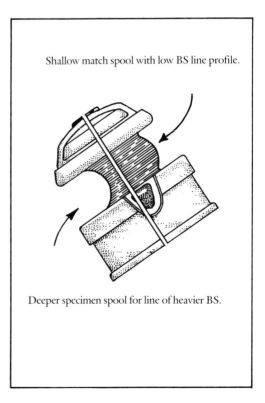

Shallow match spool with low BS line profile.

Deeper specimen spool for line of heavier BS.

Fig 15   Spool profiles.

Make and Model	Ratio	Spool Capacity
Daiwa Carbon SF1350TM	3·7:1	100m × 2lb BS
Daiwa Harrier 1657DM	5·4:1	110m × 4lb BS
Shimano SMN-M-2500X	5·2:1	120m × 2lb BS
Shimano Leger Spool		250m × 6lb BS
Shimano SSG-X 1000	5·2:1	165m × 4lb BS
Shimano BTR-GT-3500	4·6:1	300m × 8lb BS
Shimano Aerlex GTR 100	4·3:1	150m × 4lb BS
Dam CFM Match	4·1:1	100m × 3lb BS
Dam Leger Spool	5·3:1	200m × 8lb BS
Ryobi ML1C	5·3:1	290m × 4lb BS
Ryobi GR2	5·1:1	240m × 6lb BS
Mitchell 2210 RD	5·4:1	200m × 6lb BS
Mitchell 2250 RD	4·9:1	200m × 12lb BS
Silstar CX41	6·1:1	200m × 8lb BS

Table 2   Recommended reels.

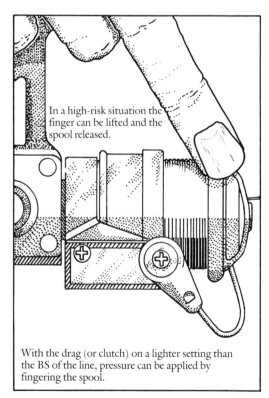

In a high-risk situation the finger can be lifted and the spool released.

With the drag (or clutch) on a lighter setting than the BS of the line, pressure can be applied by fingering the spool.

Fig 16   Spool and drag control.

introduction of new materials, most of which originate in aerospace technology. Graphite composite materials are predominant in most makes of reel today. The weight advantage is backed up by the use of non-corrodible components, which prolong durability in most circumstances. Bail arm design, with silicon carbide low-friction line rollers on 'never fail' over-centre return springs, ensures that the bail always operates at an optimum level. Skirted spools prevent tangles round the back of the spool. Spools with profiled centres – the recent Shimano Aerlex GTR, with two-speed oscillation and tapered spool is a good example – ensure that the line is laid level and even on the spool.

Many of the latest reels, particularly those produced by Shimano, have multiple-drag control systems which allow a number of pre-determined settings to be employed to suit the circumstances. A 'strike' setting allows firm hook setting with a normal midway point of clutch slip. On either side a minimum clutch setting can be selected at a flick to give line to a bolting fish, with control

Make	BS	Diameter
Drennan Specimen	1½lb (0·70kg)*	0·125mm
Drennan Specimen	2½lb (1·13kg)*	0·150mm
Drennan Specimen	3lb (1·35kg)	0·175mm
Drennan Specimen	8lb (3·60kg)	0·275mm
Drennan Specimen	10lb (4·50kg)	0·300mm
Drennan Floatfish	1·1lb (0·45kg)*	0·100mm
Drennan Floatfish	1·7lb (0·77kg)*	0·125mm
Drennan Floatfish	3·2lb (1·45kg)	0·175mm
Drennan Floatfish	5lb (2·25kg)	0·225mm
Maxima Chameleon	1lb (0·05kg)*	0·080mm
Maxima Chameleon	2lb (1·00kg)*	0·120mm
Maxima Chameleon	3lb (1.40kg)	0·150mm
Maxima Chameleon	5lb (2·40kg)	0·200mm
Maxima Chameleon	8lb (3·50kg)	0·250mm
Maxima Chameleon	10lb (4·50kg)	0·300mm
Sylcast Sorrel	1lb (0·50kg)*	0·080mm
Sylcast Sorrel	1½lb (0·70kg)*	0·090mm
Sylcast Sorrel	3lb (1·35kg)	0·100mm
Sylcast Sorrel	4lb (1·80kg)	0·170mm
Sylcast Sorrel	5lb (2·25kg)	0·200mm
Sylcast Sorrel	7lb (3.18kg)	0·250mm
Sylcast Sorrel	9lb (4.08kg)	0·300mm
Sylcast Sorrel	11lb (4.99kg)	0·320mm
	* Hooklink lines	

Table 3   Recommended monofilament lines.

applied by finger pressure on the spool, as shown in Figure 16. Finally a maximum setting allows the angler to apply pressure to slow a running fish and hold it away from snags.

The Right Reel

Listed are some of the more useful reels with their gear ratios and line capacities. As with rods, you will find that quality is accompanied by an equivalent price tag. You get what you pay for, but a compromise can be struck with reels more easily than with rods.

The best advice is to take a long hard look at as many as possible before making your choice. Do not just follow fashion; buy a reel that meets *all* your requirements.

LINES

Choice of line is just as important as the choice of rod and reel, if not more so. If you choose line of breaking strain unsuited to the action you risk breakage and disappointment either during the cast, on the strike, during the fight, or – should the fish bolt – at the net.

Matching Breaking Strain to Test Curve

Risk of breakage can be avoided if line strength is carefully matched to test curve. You can get away with exceeding the rod's maximum recommended line breaking strain, but will not find much forgiveness if you go below its minimum, so make sure to choose carefully.

Quality Line

Table 3 gives proven makes of nylon monofilament both for main lines and for suitable hook lengths for use when line of finer diameter is necessary to catch line-shy fish. Many of the specialised hook-link lines are more expensive than the bulk spooled main lines

such as Sylcast or Maxima, so it makes sense to fill your spools with one of these brands, storing hook links in smaller quantities for use as required.

With all lines an important point to bear in mind is to put enough on the reel spool to allow easy casting but not so much, however, that it spills off easily either before or during the cast. Figure 17 shows the correct level of line on a spool.

If hook links are lighter than the reel line, they should be at least 18 inches long – longer if possible – in order to provide some degree of shock-absorbing stretch and so avoid breakage.

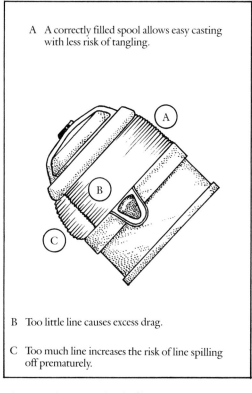

A A correctly filled spool allows easy casting with less risk of tangling.

B Too little line causes excess drag.

C Too much line increases the risk of line spilling off prematurely.

Fig 17 The correct level of line on the spool.

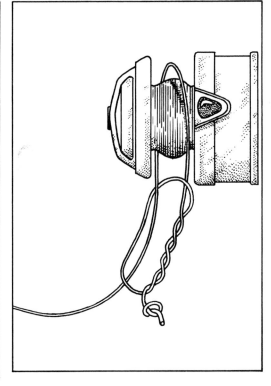

Fig 18 Spool fixing knot.

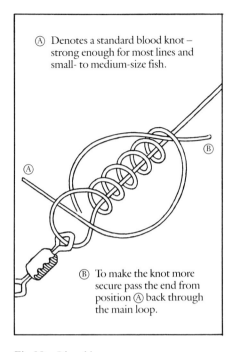

Ⓐ Denotes a standard blood knot – strong enough for most lines and small- to medium-size fish.

Ⓑ To make the knot more secure pass the end from position Ⓐ back through the main loop.

Fig 19   Blood knot.

KNOTS

Monofilament nylon line is only as strong as its weakest point, usually the knot. The useful and practical knots illustrated in Figures 18, 19, 20, 21, 22 and 23 offer high knot

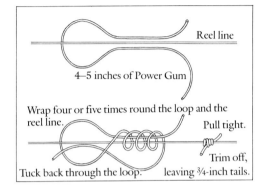

Reel line

4–5 inches of Power Gum

Wrap four or five times round the loop and the reel line.

Pull tight.

Tuck back through the loop.

Trim off, leaving ¾-inch tails.

Fig 21   Power Gum stop knot.

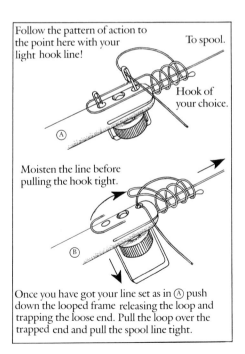

Follow the pattern of action to the point here with your light hook line!

To spool.

Hook of your choice.

Ⓐ

Moisten the line before pulling the hook tight.

Ⓑ

Once you have got your line set as in Ⓐ push down the looped frame releasing the loop and trapping the loose end. Pull the loop over the trapped end and pull the spool line tight.

Fig 20   Spade end knot.

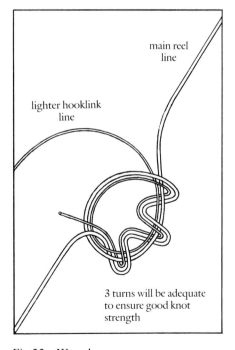

main reel line

lighter hooklink line

3 turns will be adequate to ensure good knot strength

Fig 22   Water knot.

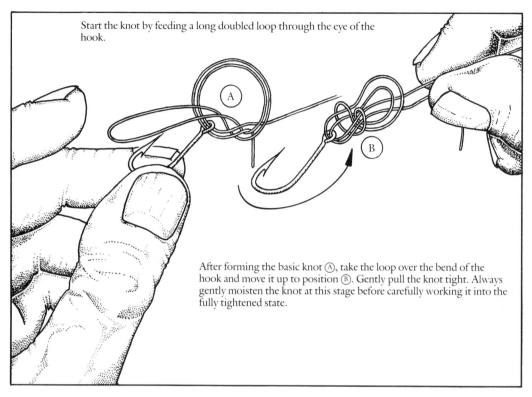

Start the knot by feeding a long doubled loop through the eye of the hook.

After forming the basic knot Ⓐ, take the loop over the bend of the hook and move it up to position Ⓑ. Gently pull the knot tight. Always gently moisten the knot at this stage before carefully working it into the fully tightened state.

Fig 23 Palomar knot, for all braided hook links.

strength. Take great care when tying all knots. It is important that they should be moistened before being fully tightened. Do not rush the tightening. If you take your time and check all is well you will get a stronger finish. It can make the difference between landing and losing that leviathan.

TERMINAL TACKLES

Of paramount importance are the terminal tackles we choose to actually hook our quarry in the first place. With the wrong terminal tackle bites may go unnoticed or – worse still – result in deep hooking. Balancing all the components down to and including the

terminal tackle will go a good way to achieving the ultimate reward of having a fairly hooked fish on the bank.

Versatile Swivel

Good swivels are one of the most important components in terminal tackle. Figure 24 illustrates three of the many types available. Of the three the most versatile is the centre one, the Diamond Eye available from Drennan Tackle. Also shown are some of the snap links which are available for use with the illustrated swivels. Again, the centre one, the Drennan Safeloc, is very useful and reliable for attaching paternoster links, leger weights, and swim feeders, and so on. Swivels can also be used

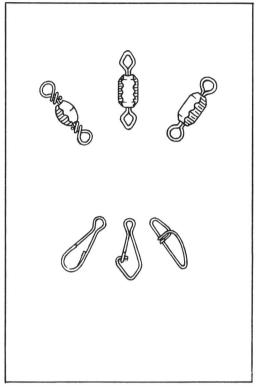

Fig 24   Assorted swivels and links.

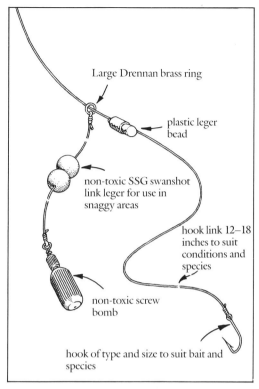

Large Drennan brass ring

plastic leger bead

non-toxic SSG swanshot link leger for use in snaggy areas

hook link 12–18 inches to suit conditions and species

non-toxic screw bomb

hook of type and size to suit bait and species

Fig 25   Assorted link leger layouts.

for sliding links and for linking reel line and hook link. It is worth covering any such links with a small piece of silicon rubber tubing to stop the line catching on – or in – any open areas.

Hook Links

An alternative of linking hook length and main line – *even if they are not of the same breaking strain* – is by twin loops or by a fixed paternoster tied with the water knot (Figure 22). Without swivels and heavy weights it is possible to use plastic leger stops like those marketed by Drennan Tackle and Gardner Tackle. These can be used with small brass rings as shown in Figure 25, to which a nylon

link and SSG weights can be added when light balanced legering is required.

HOOKS

As with rods and reels, you will eventually build up confidence in a particular make and pattern of hook, usually because of a bad experience or disappointment with another make. This addiction for one hook is very common, but many serious anglers who were once committed in this way have found that the development of specialised carp hooks has given us a wider range of hooks which suit certain species other than carp and improve capture ratio.

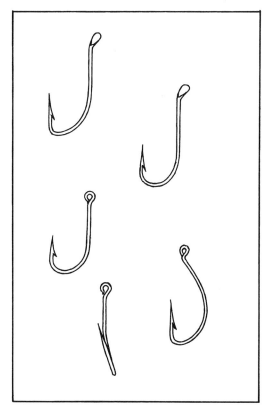

Fig 26   Assorted hook styles.

hooks for complete concealment of the hook within the caster.

Hook Choice

Bait presentation will probably dictate the size and type of hook. Baits fully mounted on the hook – luncheon meat, bread, pastes and the like – require a hook with a fairly wide gape, whilst off-hook or hair-type presentations may require smaller hooks with turned-in points. You will probably form a preference in due course but among those listed you will find a selection of reliable brands and patterns to start with.

To present boiled bottom baits and floaters off the hook with the various hair options smaller hooks may be used – from perhaps size 4 down to size 8 – on hard-fished waters. The same tactics have given rise to the development of specialist patterns to aid hooking and penetration. Try as many kinds of hook as possible and see which suits your style and methods. Remember to vary the hook to suit each method of presentation and always ensure that you are fishing with the sharpest possible hook!

Chemical Etching

Probably the single most important advance has been in the chemical etching of the points to a sharpness once only dreamt of. This new benefit has one shortcoming: the points are very easily damaged when fishing near stony areas or where hard snags exist. It pays to check the point regularly; if it is damaged, change the hook.

The second great advance is in fully closed eyes. No longer is there the risk of the line getting trapped or even cut in the gap once common on many hook eyes. Many of the smaller baits now have hooks designed specifically for them, in particular caster

BAIT MOUNTING

To mount your baits – particles, boilies or floaters – on hairs and stringers you will need a variety of needles, as shown in Figure 27, as well as a spool of very light nylon monofilament or thread for making hairs and some PVA string to secure the baits to stringers.

FLOATS

It is probably true to say that more anglers than fish are caught by floats. Look in any angler's tackle box and you will see more

Make	Model	Specification	Sizes
Mustad	Blue Match	Spade-end long shank	16–20
Drennan	Long Match	Spade-end long shank	16–20
Drennan	Carbon Feeder	Offset curved point, spade-end	10–20
Drennan	Carbon Caster	Long shank crystal bend, spade-end	16–20
Drennan	Carbon Specimen	Eyed curved point	2–18
Drennan	Super Specialist	Eyed	2–20
Partridge	Z2 Record Breaker Specialist Hook	Eyed	2–16

Table 4   Recommended hooks.

Name	Model	Sizes available
Kevin Nash	Hair-rig Hook	
Kevin Nash	Super Specialist Carp Hook	
Rod Hutchinson	Special Extra Strong Carp Hook	
Partridge	Z1 Jack Hilton Carp Hook	8–2
Partridge	Z11 Kevin Maddocks Hair-rig Hook	
Drennan	Super Specialist Hooks	
Simpson of Turnford	Carp Catcher Hooks	

Table 5   Specialist hooks.

Make	Material	Colour	BS
Masterbraid	Dacron	White	6lb, 10lb, 12lb
Sylcast	Dacron	Black	6lb, 10lb, 12lb
Berkley	Braided nylon	Camouflaged	Multiple strands of fine nylon
	Waxed dental floss		Approximately 12/15lb
	Unwaxed dental floss		Approximately 12/15lb
Kryston	Multistrand material	230 continuous strands of fibre	70lb
	Silkworm	Braided version of above	15/20lb
Kevin Nash	Gamastrand	230 continuous strands of fibre	70lb
	Gamabraid	Braided version of above	15/20lb

Table 6   Hook link materials.

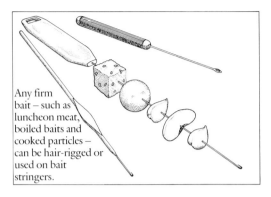

Any firm bait – such as luncheon meat, boiled baits and cooked particles – can be hair-rigged or used on bait stringers.

Fig 27   Assorted bait and stringer needles.

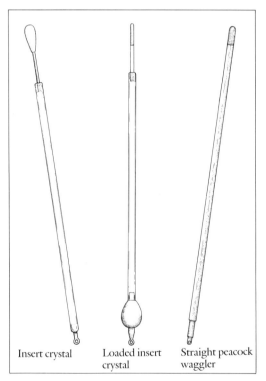

Insert crystal   Loaded insert crystal   Straight peacock waggler

Fig 28   Assorted straight-bodied floats, or wagglers.

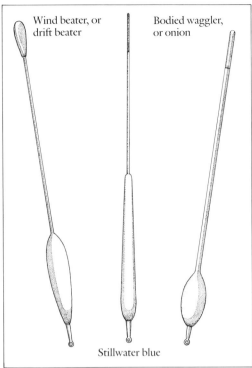

Wind beater, or drift beater

Bodied waggler, or onion

Stillwater blue

Fig 29   Assorted bodied floats, for distance and stability.

floats, and learn how to use them properly and thoroughly.

Figures 28 and 29 show a selection of useful floats for stillwater fishing. Full details of how to use them are given in the following chapters, where shotting patterns to suit various situations are also shown.

SWIMFEEDERS

An important part of fishing stillwaters, the swimfeeder helps get bait down to the bottom quickly and accurately, ensuring that the hookbait is right where the groundbait is. There are many different styles and in Figure 30 you will see a selection of the most useful,

floats that he never uses than ones he does. We all fall into the same trap at some time. Control your urges, keep a few practical

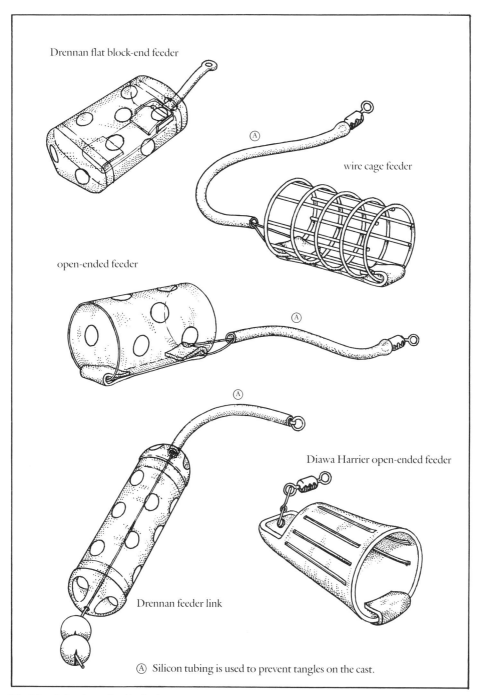

Drennan flat block-end feeder

Ⓐ

wire cage feeder

open-ended feeder

Ⓐ

Ⓐ

Diawa Harrier open-ended feeder

Drennan feeder link

Ⓐ Silicon tubing is used to prevent tangles on the cast.

Fig 30   Selection of swimfeeders.

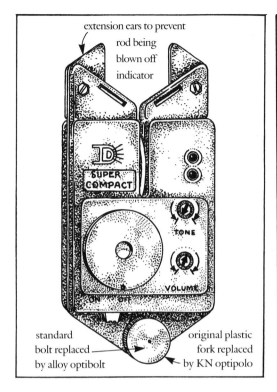

extension ears to prevent
rod being
blown off
indicator

SUPER
COMPACT

TONE

VOLUME

ON   OFF

standard
bolt replaced
by alloy optibolt

original plastic
fork replaced
by KN optipolo

Fig 31   Optonic bite indicator.

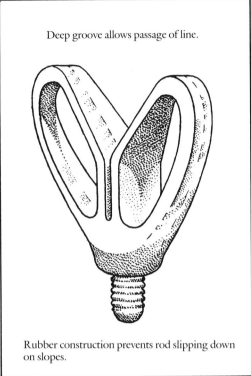

Deep groove allows passage of line.

Rubber construction prevents rod slipping down
on slopes.

Fig 32   Drennan rod-rest head.

from block-end maggot-only feeders to open-end and mesh feeders. How to use each is covered in detail in later chapters. It is worth arming yourself with a selection of these in the sizes that will suit your tackle. It is no use having swimfeeders which will weigh 3oz when full – when your rod and line can only handle 2oz for casting – something is bound to break.

BITE INDICATORS

The best of the electronic bite indicators is the Optonic illustrated in Figure 31. With its roller system it is the most sensitive in recording drop-back slack-line bites, conventional full-blooded runs and twitchy takes. The indi-

cator you choose to use will depend on your budget. Economically priced antenna-type buzzers will perform equally well in indicating full-blooded runs and twitchy takes but not drop-back-type bites. With some methods, particularly semi-fixed leads, these are very common, so choose well or save up for an Optonic-style indicator.

ROD RESTS

Whilst waiting to buy, you would be advised to purchase some of the rod-rest heads shown in Figures 32 and 33. These are essential for the free passage of the line when used with the monkey-climber-style indicator or the

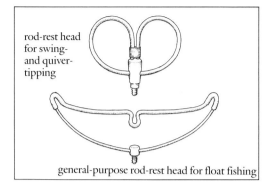

Fig 33 Rod-rest heads for float fishing and swingtipping.

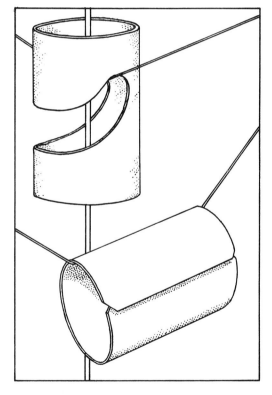

Fig 34 Tube-type bite indicators.

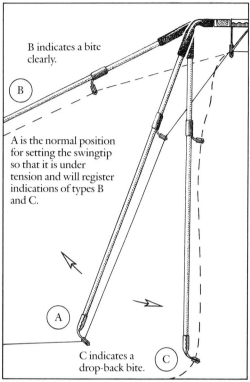

B indicates a bite clearly.

B

A is the normal position for setting the swingtip so that it is under tension and will register indications of types B and C.

A

C indicates a drop-back bite.

C

Fig 35 Swingtip indicator positions.

plastic tube indicators shown in Figure 34. These will give a good visual indication of both full takes and drop-back takes if they occur. Not every session calls for the use of audible indicators, so do not worry if you cannot afford them; use the ordinary rod rest to start with and stay with your rods.

Other bite indicators to carry will be a small selection of swingtips, quivertips, possibly some butt-type indicators and some surface bait controllers in various weights, to allow good presentation close to and away from the bank. Ensure that you have a good selection of non-toxic lead-free split shot like that made by Thamesley and Anchor Tackle, along with a selection of non-toxic lead-free leger weights.

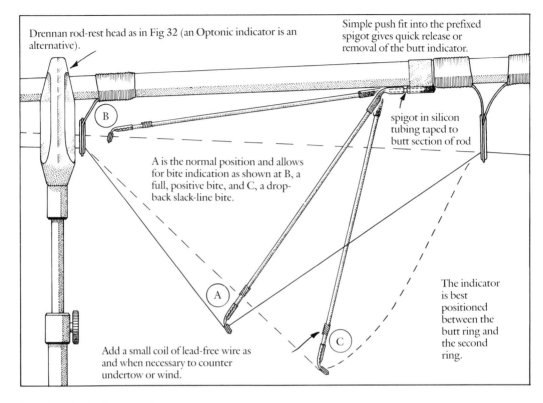

Drennan rod-rest head as in Fig 32 (an Optonic indicator is an alternative).

Simple push fit into the prefixed spigot gives quick release or removal of the butt indicator.

B

spigot in silicon tubing taped to butt section of rod

A is the normal position and allows for bite indication as shown at B, a full, positive bite, and C, a drop-back slack-line bite.

A

The indicator is best positioned between the butt ring and the second ring.

Add a small coil of lead-free wire as and when necessary to counter undertow or wind.

C

Fig 36   Butt indicator settings.

There are many other items of tackle you can accumulate and carry – we all end up carrying our own ideals. The main necessities are covered here and if you follow these basic guidelines as well as the suggestions made in the following chapters you should then be in a sound position to succeed in your task.

4 Bream
(Abramis brama)

Of all the species to be caught in stillwater the bream has enjoyed the most recent rise in popularity. This is largely the result of some exceptional catches from two waters in particular, TC pit and Queenford lagoon, both in Oxfordshire. These two waters have seen more bream of over 12lb than any other ever, with Queenford regularly producing fish of more than 15lb, with several multiple catches of fish over that weight. Despite all of these fish the current record bream did not come from Queenford but from a private Staffordshire lake. It weighed 16lb 6ozs and was caught by Tony Bromley in 1986.

There is little doubt that bigger bream could well be swimming around in pits or

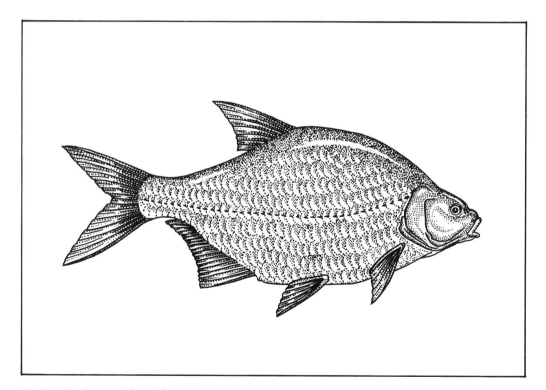

Fig 37   The bream, *Abramis brama*.

lakes throughout the country. Certainly Queenford was unknown until recently and had it not been for the exploits of anglers like Alastair Nicholson and John Knowles, who publicised their spectacular catches, we might never have known that such potential existed. It is possible that many big bream die every season without ever having seen an angler's bait.

IDENTIFICATION

The bream is easily distinguished by its deep body shape and its large black fins – particularly the big forked tail, the short-based but tall dorsal with its nine branched rays, and the very large anal fin with its 24–30 branched rays and very long base.

Depending on age and environment, the general colour may vary from a golden bronzy hue through to a deep dark bronze on older fish. Younger fish have a thick mucous coating evident on their body, which is probably one reason why a few anglers frown on the bream: it tends to cover everything it touches – landing net, keepnet and clothing. However, on the bigger, more mature specimens this mucous may be almost absent. These bigger fish have a rather coarse, scaly feel, which is far more acceptable. In either case, it is important to handle *all* bream with care: wipe off too much of the protective coating and the fish may be susceptible to disease.

SPAWNING HABITS

Spawning usually takes place between May and July, depending on water temperature and geographic location (the farther north the later). Just before and during spawning the head and flanks of the male are covered in white spawning tubercles. Spawning gives a good indication of what fish are present in a water, since the shoals that form at that time are very likely to be found on or near the shallower weedier areas of the lake or pit and a lot of rolling and splashing takes place. Most fish tend to reach spawning maturity at about 5 years, depending on the environment.

GROWTH RATE

Fish in the 3–5lb range are the most commonly caught but fish of greater weight will most certainly be present. In most lakes and gravel pits it is possible to turn up the odd individual fish of perhaps 7 or 8lb whilst fishing for roach, tench or carp. It is almost certain that the bigger fish lead a more solitary life than the smaller fish, which are usually found in large shoals.

LOCATION AND FEEDING HABITS

With recent publicity and media attention it is not surprising that the bream has to some degree become a cult fish – at least for the moment. The chances of catching one of the bigger specimens which perhaps lurk in one or more of the numerous big gravel pits dotted around the country are not great.

Of all the species, big bream can be the hardest to track down and catch. What is needed is to spend time finding a water which contains bream of the calibre you seek and then to spend as much time as possible getting to know all the intimate details of the water before you start fishing. Finally, concentrate on locating the patrol routes and ultimately the bream's feeding sites. Most of the visible sightings you will make will be of the bream moving along one of their patrol routes. Observe where they stop and watch

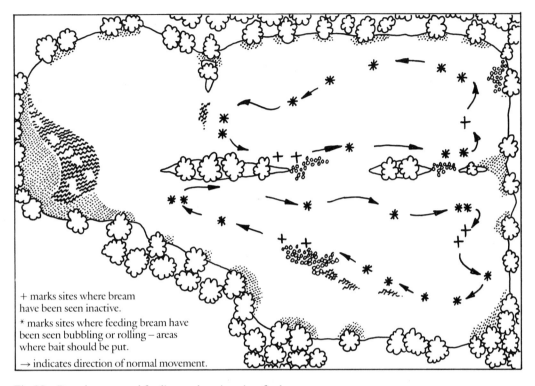

+ marks sites where bream
have been seen inactive.

* marks sites where feeding bream have
been seen bubbling or rolling – areas
where bait should be put.

→ indicates direction of normal movement.

Fig 38   Patrol routes and feeding and resting sites for bream.

closely to see if there are any signs to confirm that they have stopped to feed. There is no substitute for observation if you are to be successful at catching one of the bigger bream.

Whilst the bigger specimens of bream lead a more solitary existence their smaller brethren are by nature a shoal species and are to be found in fairly large numbers. This tends in general terms to help location since these shoal fish are usually very active in the warmer months and when on the move along one of their patrol routes they spend a lot of time priming and rolling on the surface. Again, if you are observant you will notice where this patrolling stops – it may well be one of the shoal's regular feeding sites.

A sure sign of this is either colouring up of

what may have been clear water or the appearance of large patches of small bubbles as the bream root around in the layers of silt which contain their food – perhaps bloodworm or snails. Once these areas are accurately located you can begin to try to catch your bream.

WEATHER AND SEASONAL EFFECTS

Some of the species we fish for become less active in the winter months. Not so the bream. It will usually respond to a correct and accurate baiting approach – cautious loose feeding, not heavy groundbaiting – probably in the same areas as in the warmer months. Many anglers give up trying to catch bream

White tubercles clearly visible on the head of this bream indicate that it is in condition for spawning.

A nice bag of bream taken on swimfeeder tactics from a far-bank marginal ledge.

after the end of the autumn, but there is no real justification for stopping. Remember, at one time nobody thought it was worth fishing for carp during winter, but the winter editions of the angling papers show how that myth has been exploded.

It is certainly not worth trying to catch bream in the really cold weather of winter but sport can be rewarding during periods of sustained mild weather, particularly when warm south-westerlies bring plenty of cloud and rain to stir the bream into action. Probably the best time of the winter is the closing

Dean Allen being coached by his father, Trevor, to watch his indicators at all times.

weeks of the season, especially if we have been lucky to have had a sustained warm spell.

METHODS

If you have done your groundwork by first checking that bream are actually present in the lake or gravel pit you intend fishing and, second, by doing some basic physical observation – possibly pinpointing either a regular patrol route or a holding area, depending on the time of year – then you can be confident that you stand every chance of connecting with your chosen quarry. All you need to do now is select a method that will maximise the opportunity.

Dean Allen with his first catch of bream, taken on swimfeeder maggot from a small club lake.

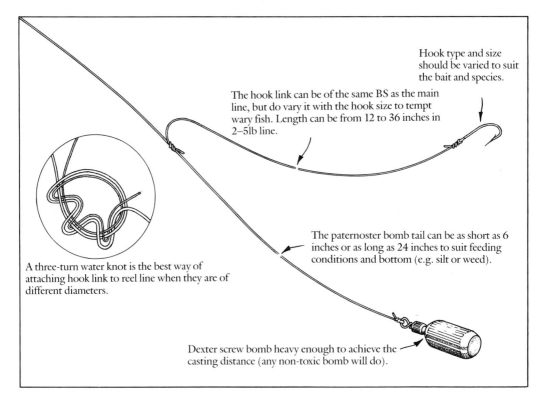

Hook type and size should be varied to suit the bait and species.

The hook link can be of the same BS as the main line, but do vary it with the hook size to tempt wary fish. Length can be from 12 to 36 inches in 2–5lb line.

The paternoster bomb tail can be as short as 6 inches or as long as 24 inches to suit feeding conditions and bottom (e.g. silt or weed).

A three-turn water knot is the best way of attaching hook link to reel line when they are of different diameters.

Dexter screw bomb heavy enough to achieve the casting distance (any non-toxic bomb will do).

Fig 39   Fixed paternoster rig.

Choosing a Method

Choice of method and terminal tackle will depend on the circumstances prevailing at the time of your visit. If you are lucky enough to arrive when bream are present and you suspect that they may actually be feeding, your choice would be to investigate the possibility of getting bites without introducing large amounts of groundbait as you would if you were attempting to attract and hold a shoal of patrolling bream.

Paternoster

The best rig in this situation is the one illustrated in Figure 39. It is a basic paternoster rig and, whilst it will allow a sound presentation of your bait, it may need some adjustment to obtain the best response. The hook link may require lengthening or shortening to suit the way the bream are feeding. The rod to use would ideally be one with a swingtip, a quivertip, or a butt indicator with perhaps an Optonic indicator. The choice should be made to suit the prevailing situation and conditions. Bait might be maggot or worm or even bread flake tipped with one of these.

Groundbaiting

A cast should be made into the feeding area to test the response, if either line bites or full-

52

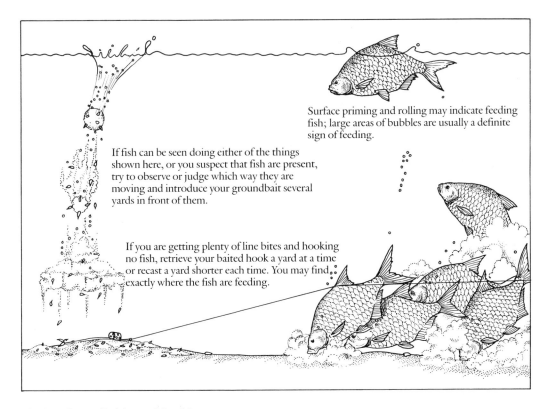

Surface priming and rolling may indicate feeding fish; large areas of bubbles are usually a definite sign of feeding.

If fish can be seen doing either of the things shown here, or you suspect that fish are present, try to observe or judge which way they are moving and introduce your groundbait several yards in front of them.

If you are getting plenty of line bites and hooking no fish, retrieve your baited hook a yard at a time or recast a yard shorter each time. You may find exactly where the fish are feeding.

Fig 40   Groundbaiting and line bites.

blooded bites are forthcoming it may not be necessary to introduce heavy amounts of groundbait, but it would be beneficial to begin a light feeding programme to hold the bream. Many anglers fishing for bream, start by mixing and introducing large quantities of groundbait. If you did this in our hypothetical situation you would more than likely drive the fish out of the swim. Very few fish would tolerate heavy amounts of feed being dropped on their heads. It is best to introduce your groundbait slightly outside and to one side of the feeding area. Use a loose fairly dry mix to allow it to break up easily and be carried down to the bottom just in front of the feeding bream.

You may of course arrive at your swim and find no signs of bream activity. In this case it is best to make an exploratory series of casts to check; it is always possible that fish are in residence and heavy groundbaiting might drive them away. If no bites or line bites occur it is all right to feed in your groundbait. Do not put it all in at once but build it up slowly, either by hand or by swimfeeder.

Swimfeeders

If you decide to use a swimfeeder you have the choice between the types shown in Figures 43 and 46, either an open-ended feeder or a cage feeder. The open end will require a dryish groundbait mix to form the two end plugs, with maggots or hemp and

A nice bag of bream for the author, the sort of catch that comes from accurate location and good bait presentation.

A bream from Ballycuirke Lake, Moycullen, Co. Galway, comes to the net.

casters in between. The cage feeder can be used in a similar way but maggots are best left out of your groundbait, which should again be a fairly dry mix with the hemp, casters and hookbait samples already mixed in. Drop the feeder into the mix, squeeze some groundbait into the mesh and cast it into the swim.

Hookbaits

If you have got the mix correct, shortly after casting and settling on the bottom the groundbait plugs on the open-end feeder will dissolve, allowing the bait out. With the cage feeder the feed will deposit itself on the bottom. Fish hookbaits of either of the free offerings or bread, worms, or cocktails. If you are using bread flake on the hook, include some pinches of flake in your groundbait, whether delivered loose or with a feeder. Bites will eventually be forthcoming. Regular recasting will slowly build up the groundbait and any flavourings and attractors will carry on any undertow and draw fish into your well

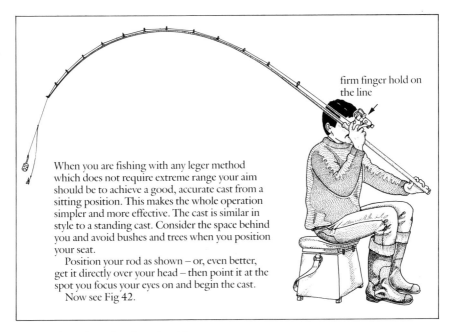

firm finger hold on the line

When you are fishing with any leger method which does not require extreme range your aim should be to achieve a good, accurate cast from a sitting position. This makes the whole operation simpler and more effective. The cast is similar in style to a standing cast. Consider the space behind you and avoid bushes and trees when you position your seat.

Position your rod as shown – or, even better, get it directly over your head – then point it at the spot you focus your eyes on and begin the cast.

Now see Fig 42.

Fig 41   Seated overhead casting (1).

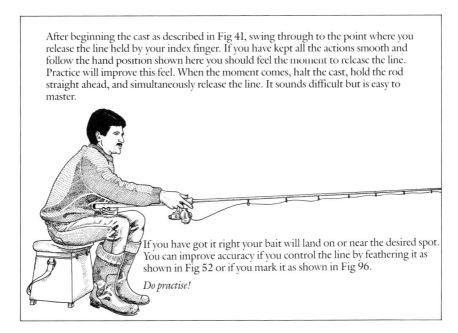

After beginning the cast as described in Fig 41, swing through to the point where you release the line held by your index finger. If you have kept all the actions smooth and follow the hand position shown here you should feel the moment to release the line. Practice will improve this feel. When the moment comes, halt the cast, hold the rod straight ahead, and simultaneously release the line. It sounds difficult but is easy to master.

If you have got it right your bait will land on or near the desired spot. You can improve accuracy if you control the line by feathering it as shown in Fig 52 or if you mark it as shown in Fig 96.

Do practise!

Fig 42   Seated overhead casting (2).

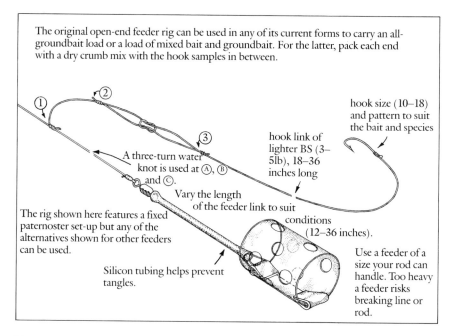

The original open-end feeder rig can be used in any of its current forms to carry an all-groundbait load or a load of mixed bait and groundbait. For the latter, pack each end with a dry crumb mix with the hook samples in between.

hook size (10–18) and pattern to suit the bait and species

hook link of lighter BS (3–5lb), 18–36 inches long

A three-turn water knot is used at Ⓐ, Ⓑ and Ⓒ.

Vary the length of the feeder link to suit conditions (12–36 inches).

The rig shown here features a fixed paternoster set-up but any of the alternatives shown for other feeders can be used.

Silicon tubing helps prevent tangles.

Use a feeder of a size your rod can handle. Too heavy a feeder risks breaking line or rod.

Fig 43   Open-end feeder rig.

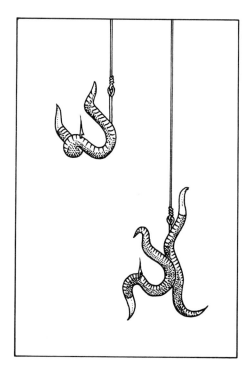

Fig 44   Brandlings on the hook.

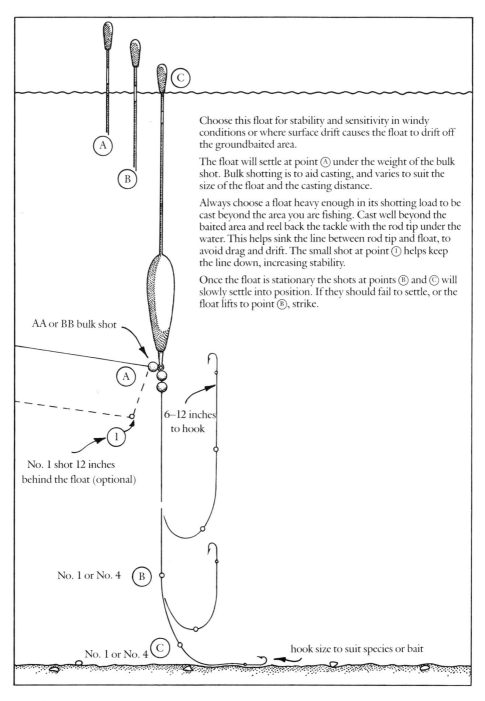

Choose this float for stability and sensitivity in windy conditions or where surface drift causes the float to drift off the groundbaited area.

The float will settle at point Ⓐ under the weight of the bulk shot. Bulk shotting is to aid casting, and varies to suit the size of the float and the casting distance.

Always choose a float heavy enough in its shotting load to be cast beyond the area you are fishing. Cast well beyond the baited area and reel back the tackle with the rod tip under the water. This helps sink the line between rod tip and float, to avoid drag and drift. The small shot at point ① helps keep the line down, increasing stability.

Once the float is stationary the shots at points Ⓑ and Ⓒ will slowly settle into position. If they should fail to settle, or the float lifts to point Ⓑ, strike.

AA or BB bulk shot

6–12 inches to hook

No. 1 shot 12 inches behind the float (optional)

No. 1 or No. 4 Ⓑ

No. 1 or No. 4 Ⓒ

hook size to suit species or bait

Fig 45   Wind or drift beater float rig.

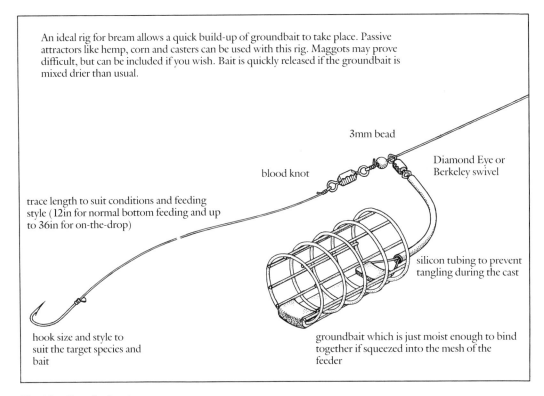

An ideal rig for bream allows a quick build-up of groundbait to take place. Passive attractors like hemp, corn and casters can be used with this rig. Maggots may prove difficult, but can be included if you wish. Bait is quickly released if the groundbait is mixed drier than usual.

3mm bead

blood knot

Diamond Eye or Berkeley swivel

trace length to suit conditions and feeding style (12in for normal bottom feeding and up to 36in for on-the-drop)

silicon tubing to prevent tangling during the cast

hook size and style to suit the target species and bait

groundbait which is just moist enough to bind together if squeezed into the mesh of the feeder

Fig 46   Cage feeder rig.

fed swim. Any patrolling fish should be able to find it and sport should begin.

Alternative Methods

When bites do come it is important to try changing the hook and feeder-link lengths to optimise bite indication. It may also be beneficial to try using a fixed paternoster link to attach the feeder instead of the free-running rig as illustrated, or to use a block-end or feeder link with maggots only inside. It will depend on circumstances and conditions, the weather and the time of year.

5 Carp
(Cyprinus carpio)

Of all the species that inhabit the lakes, pits and reservoirs we fish it is the carp in its various forms that nowadays receives the greatest attention both in fishery management terms and from us anglers. There are anglers who deny the attraction of this fish, but once they are connected to one by rod and line – either by design or by chance – there is no turning back; the appeal is inescapable.

So it is not surprising that there has been a growth in fisheries catering for this growing interest. There has also been a parallel growth in fish farms seeking to produce larger and faster-growing carp to supply the demand. The carp is not indigenous to the British Isles.

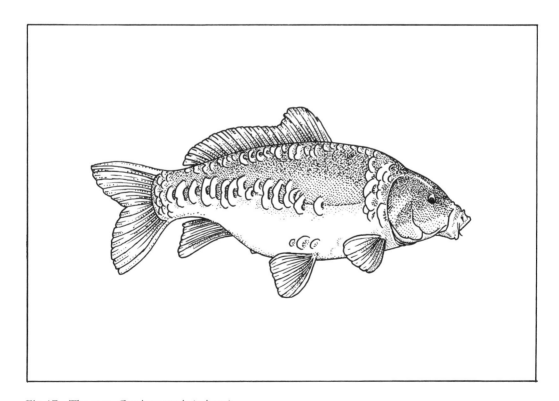

Fig 47   The carp, *Cyprinus carpio* (mirror).

It was introduced to English waters between the thirteenth and fifteenth centuries by monks from the Continent. They brought the carp with them as a food supply and constructed stewponds for the purposes of rearing and growing them purely for the table.

IDENTIFICATION

These fish we know as the original wild carp and they are a different strain from the fish you will come to experience in carp fisheries. They are similar in all the basic features: large extendable mouth with two barbels on either side, one small barbel on each side of the upper lip and a much longer one in the back fold of the upper lip; the large concave dorsal fin, which is long-based with between 17 and 22 branched rays with a strong toothed spine at the front. This spine has a serrated edge, which can foul in the mesh of keepnets, which is the main reason for *not* retaining carp in them. The general colouring is the same, though there are local variations. The original strain of wild carp, however, varies in its overall size compared with the present cultivated strains. Wild common carp very rarely exceed ten pounds, with the majority of fish only reaching three to four pounds. Wild carp waters are hard to find and when you find one it will invariably contain a high number of carp in this small size range, though there is always the chance of a bigger fish lurking around, and what the smaller fish lack in size they will make up for in the spectacular way they fight once hooked. If the opportunity comes your way to fish for them, seize it.

The need for good table fish on the Continent – particularly in Hungary, Czechoslovakia and Germany – led fish farmers in those countries to set about cultivating a new strain of fish, of greater size and growth rate and also with few or no scales. This strain of fish has come to be known as king carp, and these are the fish – in one of three forms, fully scaled, mirror and leather – that we fish for today. There are various other subgroups – such as linear, plated and scattered-scale mirrors – which makes fish identification more varied. The different strains also vary in shape, from the long, muscular Galician to the dumpy, rounded Italian strain.

The Galician strain gave us our two recent record fish, more commonly known by the importers name of Leney. Both were stocked as fingerlings in Redmire Pool back in the early 1950s. These fish are Dick Walker's fully-scaled common of 44lb and Chris Yates's current record mirror carp of 51lb 6oz, caught in the opening weeks of the 1980 season.

SPAWNING HABITS

In their natural environment carp usually spawn in late May or early June, depending on weather and water temperature (which are sometimes not stable until July). The eggs, of which each female will produce many hundreds of thousands, are laid in shallow water amongst weed and reedbeds and usually hatch in 3–8 days. Whilst a lot of the eggs will hatch and grow, there is a tendency for carp to eat a lot of their own spawn. Of those which survive to grow into their first year a fair percentage die as a result of unsuitable temperatures and other factors. Predation by perch and pike, where they are present, takes a heavy toll.

LOCATION AND FEEDING HABITS

There are many factors in catching carp, and understanding their habits, likes and dislikes is of the greatest importance if you are to be successful. Location of carp of all sizes depends on your ability to read the water and identify the features and areas that the carp will frequent, be it to feed, or to rest, or simply areas along a patrol route where the carp may browse for a few moments in search of a new feeding site.

One theme runs through all the chapters on the various species – the chance of catching is greatest if your baited hook is presented where the fish will *feed*. On all the waters you visit you are likely to find numerous areas which are feeding or safe sites – it could be on a marginal shelf on deep lakes or pits, a gravel bar on one of the big pits or lakes, the margins of an ordinary shallow lake, among weedbeds or reedbeds. The most positive way to locate carp feeding sites is by watching and actually seeing them feeding, or, if you suspect they feed in a particular area but are unable to see, try placing some bait samples in the chosen area and checking if they are still there 24 hours later (or sooner if you are desperate).

Things to look for are patches of bubbles fizzing to the surface, or areas of coloured water, or fish rolling in or over certain areas on a regular basis – or a combination of all three. Regular observation before fishing and a detailed map showing the appropriate features – shallow areas, deep areas, gullies, bars, snags, weedbeds, and so on – are very important. In this way you will be able to build up a picture of where and when the carp will be according to weather conditions. The direction of wind can be very important since a

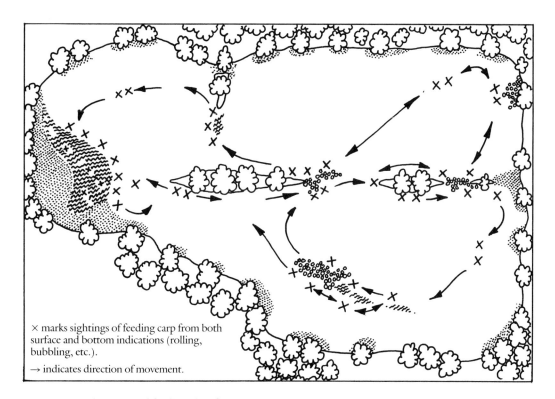

× marks sightings of feeding carp from both surface and bottom indications (rolling, bubbling, etc.).

→ indicates direction of movement.

Fig 48   Patrol routes and feeding sites for carp.

Alan Drury enjoys the thrill of playing a surface-hooked carp on a soft-actioned rod, at close range.

A super near-linear mirror of 15lb for the author, taken on surface-fished crust tight in the margins.

The author at ease playing a surface-hooked carp. In this short 4-hour session the author and Alan Drury hooked twelve fish while the other anglers went fishless on bottom baits.

Alan Drury displays the carp hooked and played in the previous shot. The successful bait was surface-fished chum mixer fished off a Ten Pin controller.

bank subject to the effects of a prevailing wind for more than 24 hours will be the area most likely to see carp feeding on food items blown there on the wind as well as items of natural food released by wave action on the margins and their subsequent distribution by the wind-induced undertow. Islands and gravel bars can also be affected in the same way, so give them a try as well.

On heavily fished waters where carp are under pressure there will be periods when the carp will be well away from the disturbance of anglers, perhaps in deep water or among thick weedbeds. However, if the water sees less activity at dusk and through the dark hours it is highly likely that the carp will move back into the margins to clear up bait left by the departed anglers. If you take time to watch for this you will be able to capitalise on some relatively easy fishing, so be observant.

WEATHER AND SEASONAL EFFECTS

One of the most influential forces on carp fishing can be the wind. It can chill a water, and it can generate a higher oxygen content by wave action, which creates marginal disturbances. All this can influence feeding, as can high and low temperatures or sudden change in temperature either up or down. Warm summer weather can induce surface activity, with fish cruising just under the surface, or it can make the fish lethargic and encourage them to seek sanctuary and shade in weed or lily beds.

Depending on temperature, winter can be as productive as summer, if not more so. There used to be a belief that carp hibernated in the bottom mud and silt from October to March. That theory has been completely destroyed in recent years, with some tremendous catches of carp in midwinter. The most productive winter fishing is during periods of milder weather; all forms of fishing are of course impossible when the lakes are frozen over. Choose to fish when there is a warm westerly weather front with plenty of wind and rain. This type of weather is sure to induce some feeding activity among the carp population.

Location of Carp in Winter

Start by fishing areas where weedbeds grow in summer and areas which are known summer hot spots or feeding areas. Once you locate them you may well find the winter hot spot and you may be able to capitalise on some tremendous sport. If you intend trying some serious winter carping, once you have noted likely areas of winter activity a programme of regular bait introduction – at least a couple of baitings each week – will be necessary to give the carp a source of winter feed on which they might become dependent, to your advantage!

METHODS

Methods for catching carp vary according to circumstances. First you need to identify the size and type of carp you are fishing for. If the fishery is newly stocked with fish of smaller size, running up to double figures, or if it is a heavily stocked or overstocked water, it may not be necessary to resort to super-sophisticated terminal tackle. There is absolutely no need to complicate your fishing unnecessarily. Start with the simple methods and advance towards the more complex as and when you need to – and when you have come to understand how, why and where the methods work.

Once you have located where the carp are feeding, you must consider which method will suit the requirements of fishing the margin

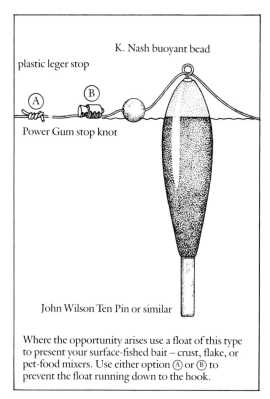

K. Nash buoyant bead

plastic leger stop

(A)   (B)

Power Gum stop knot

John Wilson Ten Pin or similar

Where the opportunity arises use a float of this type
to present your surface-fished bait – crust, flake, or
pet-food mixers. Use either option (A) or (B) to
prevent the float running down to the hook.

Fig 49 Surface bait presentation with an
original John Wilson Ten Pin.

or at close to medium range, both on the
bottom and possibly on the surface. Whether
with freelined, float-fished or legered bait, the
important thing is to choose a combination of
bait and method which will give the best
results in the given situation.

Freelining

Of all methods the simplest surely must be the
freelined bait, since the only thing you have
on the line is the hook. You can freeline for
both bottom- and surface-fishing up to a
reasonable range, but it is most practical at
one or two rod lengths.

Freelined surface baits are for use when you
can see your quarry patrolling or feeding in
marginal weed or lily beds. On warm, bright
days it is not unusual to find carp cruising at
the surface or lying under or between lily
leaves and these fish can be tempted by careful
presentation of either bread flake or bread
crust. A piece of either lightly dunked in the
margin will carry sufficient weight for short
casts. With no weight or float, the bait will
drop into place without too much disturbance and is less likely to snag during the playing of a hooked carp since there the line is
unencumbered by anything but the hook.

The best tackle for this sort of fishing is a
compound-action rod with a test curve of
$1\frac{1}{2}$–2lb and 8–12lb line. Hook size depends
on bait size, but always choose a strong
forged brand such as the Drennan Super
Specimen or similar. With surface fishing you
usually watch the bait for bite indication, but
if you are fishing at dusk or concentrating on
another rod then a simple bobbin combined
with an audible indicator such as an Optonic
will make a lot of sense.

Freelining bottom baits is a bit more difficult, but if the opportunity should present
itself then make use of it. A likely situation is
where you can see fish feeding, perhaps along
a marginal shelf or in a shallow area of the
lake. The greatest challenge is getting into a
position to allow good presentation without
scaring the feeding fish. If you can see that the
fish is moving slowly along in a specific direction, set yourself up a few yards or so in front
of its paths and get a bait into position.
Maggot, worm, bread, sweetcorn, or a soft
paste are baits that you might try. It might be
necessary for good presentation to add a BB
or AA shot to hold down the line above the
hook. Bite indication will probably be by
sight of the bait being taken. The time to
strike is the moment you see the bait moving
into the carp's mouth – any delay can see the
bait ejected before you can strike. Alterna-

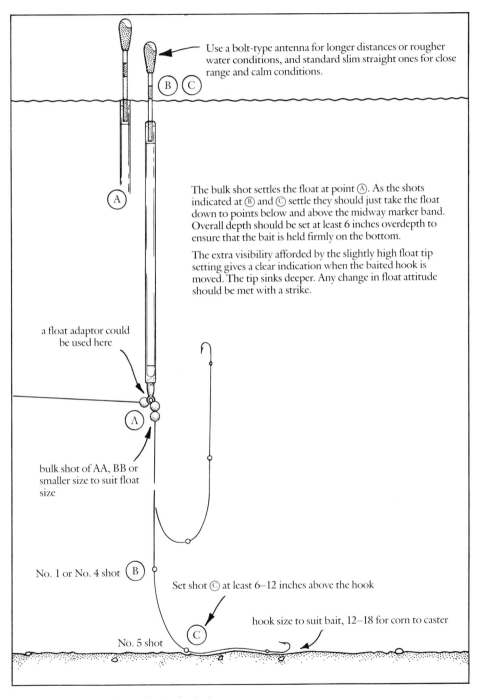

Use a bolt-type antenna for longer distances or rougher water conditions, and standard slim straight ones for close range and calm conditions.

The bulk shot settles the float at point Ⓐ. As the shots indicated at Ⓑ and Ⓒ settle they should just take the float down to points below and above the midway marker band. Overall depth should be set at least 6 inches overdepth to ensure that the bait is held firmly on the bottom.

The extra visibility afforded by the slightly high float tip setting gives a clear indication when the baited hook is moved. The tip sinks deeper. Any change in float attitude should be met with a strike.

a float adaptor could be used here

bulk shot of AA, BB or smaller size to suit float size

No. 1 or No. 4 shot Ⓑ

Set shot Ⓒ at least 6–12 inches above the hook

hook size to suit bait, 12–18 for corn to caster

No. 5 shot

Fig 50   Insert crystal waggler rig for laying on.

In some circumstances you will need to make
long casts. The overhead cast meets this need.
Standing gives you extra power to make the
distance.

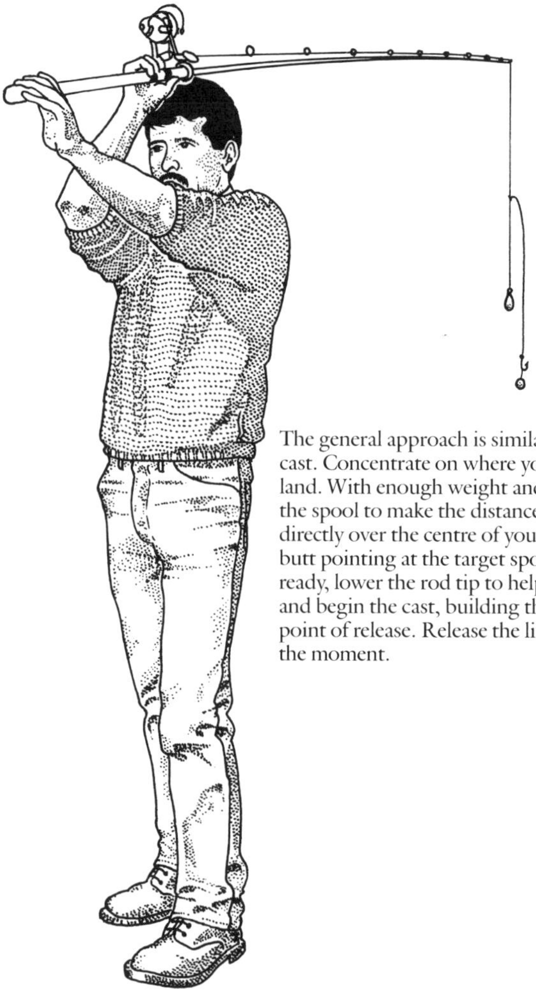

The general approach is similar to the seated
cast. Concentrate on where you want the bait to
land. With enough weight and enough line on
the spool to make the distance, position the rod
directly over the centre of your head with the
butt pointing at the target spot. When you are
ready, lower the rod tip to help compress the rod
and begin the cast, building the power to the
point of release. Release the line when you feel
the moment.

The position of the feet will have a significant
effect on the way the cast develops.

Control of distance can be achieved by
feathering, as shown in Fig 52.

Fig 51 · Overhead casting – standing.

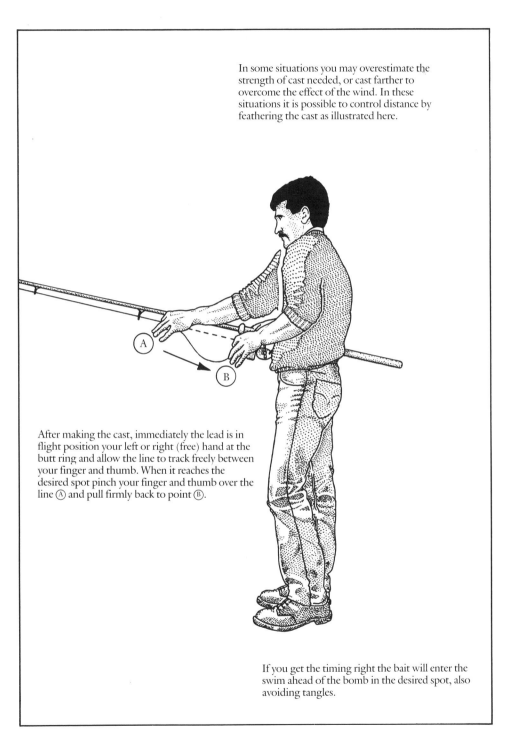

In some situations you may overestimate the strength of cast needed, or cast farther to overcome the effect of the wind. In these situations it is possible to control distance by feathering the cast as illustrated here.

After making the cast, immediately the lead is in flight position your left or right (free) hand at the butt ring and allow the line to track freely between your finger and thumb. When it reaches the desired spot pinch your finger and thumb over the line Ⓐ and pull firmly back to point Ⓑ.

If you get the timing right the bait will enter the swim ahead of the bomb in the desired spot, also avoiding tangles.

Fig 52   Feathering the cast.

Float Fishing

tively, watch the line where it enters the water or where it leaves the rod tip and strike as the line begins to move along the surface.

A development of freelining is the use of a small float to create some surface indication. The bait itself may provide enough casting weight or an AA or swanshot (SSG) may be attached. Shot can either be fished overdepth, with the float flat on the surface, or as you might with a 'lift method' set-up as illustrated in Figure 88. The most practical type of float is a piece of colour-tipped peacock quill attached by a small piece of silicon rubber tubing. Use a float of a length to balance the

shot (see Figure 90). This rig can be used for all close-to-medium-range bottom fishing with any bait you might choose. The great advantage is that you can fish simply, adjusting the float to depth or fishing it overdepth and just tightening the line enough to cock the float.

Tackle for this type of fishing is best decided on with the size of fish being taken into consideration. For small-fish waters a good-quality compound-action float rod of 12–13 feet combined with lines of 4–6lb BS will suffice. On big-fish waters a compound-action carp rod of 1½lb test curve, about 11–12 feet long, with lines of 7–9lb BS, will serve better.

When fishing at close range, either freeline

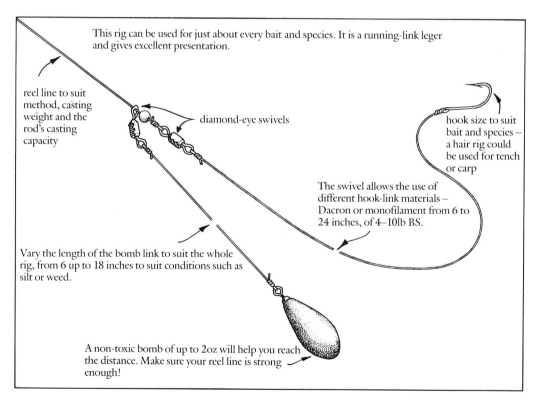

This rig can be used for just about every bait and species. It is a running-link leger and gives excellent presentation.

reel line to suit method, casting weight and the rod's casting capacity

diamond-eye swivels

hook size to suit bait and species – a hair rig could be used for tench or carp

The swivel allows the use of different hook-link materials – Dacron or monofilament from 6 to 24 inches, of 4–10lb BS.

Vary the length of the bomb link to suit the whole rig, from 6 up to 18 inches to suit conditions such as silt or weed.

A non-toxic bomb of up to 2oz will help you reach the distance. Make sure your reel line is strong enough!

Fig 53   Running paternoster rig.

or float, it is vital to set the clutch or drag correctly. If a good fish takes off from close range it is wise to let it take line off the clutch rather than attempt to back-wind, which risks breakage and disappointment.

Legering

Many of the different publicised legering methods will catch carp; likewise, the situations to which they are suited also differ widely. A lot of them are unsuitable and, quite honestly, unnecessary for most run-of-the-mill carp-fishing situations. If you are fishing well to overstocked waters you will find that one or two of the basic rigs detailed throughout this book for some of the other species will catch just as well as the 'super' rigs. However, the requirements of good bait presentation demand efficient tackle, and you will find in the two rigs that follow the sort of qualities that will ensure that you get your bait where you want it and can be confident that bait presentation and hooking potential are at their best.

The first rig, illustrated in Figure 53, is a running paternoster. Basically, it comprises two tails, one carrying the hook and the other the chosen leger weight. The length of hook link and bomb link are varied to suit given feeding and environmental situations. Preoccupied feeding over a hard gravel bottom in the early season might require both lengths being short – for example, a hook link 4 inches with the bomb at 2 inches. A soft bottom might require a longer bomb link of perhaps 12 inches or more. Late-season shy-biting carp may require a basic confidence rig with a hook link of up to 24 inches and a bomb link of 12 inches on hard bottoms or even 24 inches over silt. It is a case of knowing your water and reading the signs.

If you are not getting bites on a known good bait it could be that you are fishing over

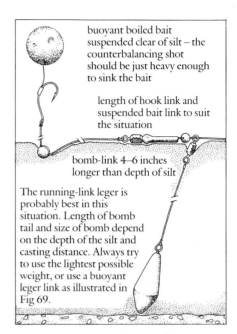

buoyant boiled bait suspended clear of silt – the counterbalancing shot should be just heavy enough to sink the bait

length of hook link and suspended bait link to suit the situation

bomb-link 4–6 inches longer than depth of silt

The running-link leger is probably best in this situation. Length of bomb tail and size of bomb depend on the depth of the silt and casting distance. Always try to use the lightest possible weight, or use a buoyant leger link as illustrated in Fig 69.

Fig 54   A buoyant bait over silt.

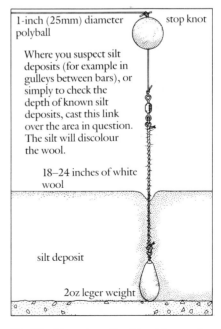

1-inch (25mm) diameter polyball

stop knot

Where you suspect silt deposits (for example in gulleys between bars), or simply to check the depth of known silt deposits, cast this link over the area in question. The silt will discolour the wool.

18–24 inches of white wool

silt deposit

2oz leger weight

Fig 55   Detecting silt with white wool.

Alan Drury carefully returns a nice carp to the water after carrying it back in the weigh sling to save the fish from being dropped and damaged.

The result of a short 4-hour session – a low-double-figure carp for the author.

weed or silt and the bait is being obscured. The answer is to use an absorbent type of bait, such as a boiled bait. After casting into your swim leave the bait for some time, then retrieve and check its smell. If it has been in a bad situation it may well smell rotten and look dirty.

Another method of checking for silt is to attach a 24-inch length of white wool to a 1½–2oz bomb, slide a 1-inch polyball on the reel line, join reel line and wool together and tie a stop for the polyball at about 4 feet. Cast the rig into the area where you suspect there is silt and the depth of the silt will show as a black stain on the white wool. If silt is present try adjusting the length of the bomb tail until either you stop getting soured baits or the bites start coming. A buoyant off-bottom bait will be very useful in a swim where there is any risk of the bait being lost in silt.

Another efficient and popular rig is the

semi-fixed paternoster which can fairly be described as a 'bolt rig'. This is more useful on hard-fished waters where the carp are more educated to both anglers' baits and rigs. You may only get one opportunity to hook the fish and this type of rig certainly helps. Apply the same principles of tail length to suit bottom conditions and feeding patterns. In some situations this rig needs to be combined with bolt-effect bait mounting – side-mounted or hair-rigged boiled or particle baits – to maximise on the chance of hooking carp after they have been tempted to take your bait. Figure 56 shows the layout of an efficient semi-fixed rig.

These methods work efficiently at short-to-medium ranges and at a push could, in the shorter link lengths, work well at reasonably long ranges. Legering is a vast subject and more detailed discussion can be found in some of the books recommended in Further Reading. May I particularly recommend my own *Introduction to Carp Fishing*.

A nice example of a mirror carp taken on peanut from a small gravel pit by Dave Wilson.

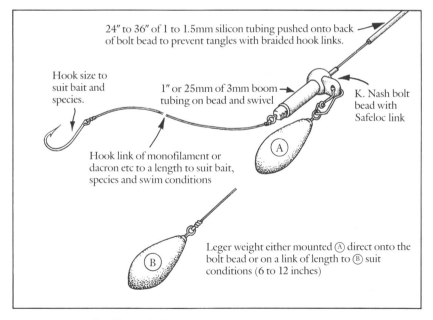

Hook size to suit bait and species.

24″ to 36″ of 1 to 1.5mm silicon tubing pushed onto back of bolt bead to prevent tangles with braided hook links.

1″ or 25mm of 3mm boom tubing on bead and swivel

K. Nash bolt bead with Safeloc link

Hook link of monofilament or dacron etc to a length to suit bait, species and swim conditions

Ⓐ

Ⓑ

Leger weight either mounted Ⓐ direct onto the bolt bead or on a link of length to Ⓑ suit conditions (6 to 12 inches)

Fig (56)   Semi-fixed leger (bolt rig)

71

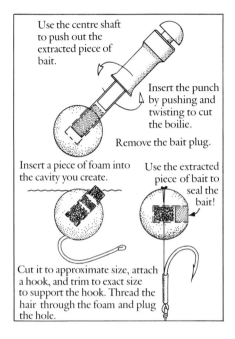

Use the centre shaft to push out the extracted piece of bait.

Insert the punch by pushing and twisting to cut the boilie.

Remove the bait plug.

Insert a piece of foam into the cavity you create.

Use the extracted piece of bait to seal the bait!

Cut it to approximate size, attach a hook, and trim to exact size to support the hook. Thread the hair through the foam and plug the hole.

Fig 57   Marvic buoyant boilie punch.

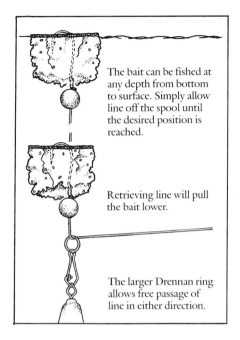

The bait can be fished at any depth from bottom to surface. Simply allow line off the spool until the desired position is reached.

Retrieving line will pull the bait lower.

The larger Drennan ring allows free passage of line in either direction.

Fig 59   Legered crust.

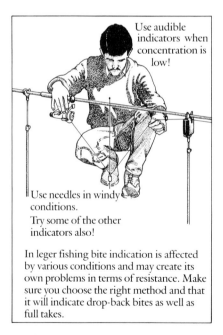

Use audible indicators when concentration is low!

Use needles in windy conditions.
Try some of the other indicators also!

In leger fishing bite indication is affected by various conditions and may create its own problems in terms of resistance. Make sure you choose the right method and that it will indicate drop-back bites as well as full takes.

Fig 58   Bite indicator settings.

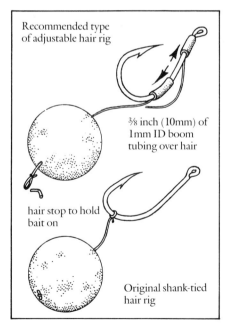

Recommended type of adjustable hair rig

3/8 inch (10mm) of 1mm ID boom tubing over hair

hair stop to hold bait on

Original shank-tied hair rig

Fig 60   Hair rig layouts.

Rod and line requirements will be met by the short-range tackle suggested for bigger carp. Float rods do not make good leger rods so, if you are going to practise legering for carp or any of the larger species, it is worth buying some suitable tackle. Longer-range fishing calls for stronger tackle, both for casting and for controlling hooked fish. Lack of power will almost undoubtedly result in disappointment for the angler and possible suffering for the fish.

To close this section on carp, there are two medium-range methods which will undoubtedly help you catch carp. They are both surface methods, one static and the other mobile. The first involves legering a floating bait in a known feeding or patrol area both on the surface or at any level from surface down to the lake or pit bottom. Figure 59 shows it in detail.

The mobile approach is achieved by the use of a self-cocking float. There are numerous patterns available in tackle shops so you will find no difficulty in obtaining one. The float is used in conjunction with a long hook link. Figure 49 shows the rig in detail. Baiting is similar to bottom particle fishing, in that you introduce fairly large quantities of floating baits (Pedigree Chum mixer, Go Cat) or floating boiled baits to get the carp preoccupied before you introduce your hook sample. On

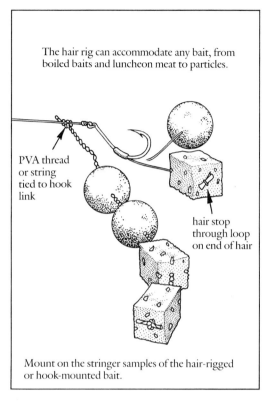

The hair rig can accommodate any bait, from boiled baits and luncheon meat to particles.

PVA thread or string tied to hook link

hair stop through loop on end of hair

Mount on the stringer samples of the hair-rigged or hook-mounted bait.

Fig 61   Hair-rigged bait with a stringer.

good days this method will outfish bottom baits totally. The baits can be attached direct to the hook or to a hair loop on the back of the hook.

6 Perch (Perca fluviatilis)

Few young anglers – or adults – will have failed to catch a small perch during their early attempts at fishing stillwaters. Float-fished maggot or worm close into lily beds and weedbeds are usually guaranteed to produce a sample of the juvenile fish of this species in the early months of the season. Those seeking to catch better-quality specimens will need to wait till the autumn and early winter for a good chance of catching, as this is the time when you will witness the scattering roach and rudd fry shoals, which are robbed of their sanctuary as the weedbeds start to die back. In seasons when warm weather encourages roach and other species to spawn early fry activity can be seen throughout the late summer as well.

Fig 62   The perch, *Perca fluviatilis*.

IDENTIFICATION

A very distinctive fish, the perch is relatively deep in the body with a short, well-rounded head and almost cavernous mouth, which the perch willingly fills with the biggest dead or live prey it can catch. A point worth remembering when fishing for big perch with deadbaits is that they have a distinct liking for fresh deadbaits, and particularly small perch.

The two dorsal fins, though separate, are extremely close together at their bases. The front dorsal fin has between 13 and 16 spines. They can cause the angler some discomfort if not handled correctly. The answer is to smooth the front dorsal down by sliding the hand down from the head and over the fin instead of trying to grab hold of the fish around the middle. The second dorsal has one spine and from 13 to 16 rays.

The texture of the perch's scales is very distinctive. They give the fish a very coarse feel and the scales covering the gill covers are very sharp-edged.

The colouring of the perch is very vivid. The body is boldly marked with dark, almost black bars on an olive-green and gold backcloth, lightening on the underbelly to white. The tail, anal and pelvic fins are bright red in colour. Note that the pelvic fins are much farther forward, almost directly under the pectoral fins, which are olive-green and brown to match the rest of the body.

SPAWNING HABITS

Spawning takes place from April to May, depending on water temperatures. The fish spawn in small shoals amongst weedbeds, and the eggs are laid in a lacy mat over weed, twigs, and the like around the margins. Hatching is usually completed in about eight days so long as the water temperature remains stable at approximately 13 degrees centigrade.

As they grow the young fry feed on planktonic crustaceans and then move on to insect larvae and small fish fry of other species. As they grow in size the shoal style of life is dropped in favour of a more solitary existence. Many fish seem to attain a rather moderate size and fail to grow into bigger specimens. Many perch fail to grow beyond 4–6oz; many that do seem to suffer from ulcers and sores and it is possible that many die soon afterwards.

In recent years we have witnessed a healthier run of perch with a good number of fish growing to weights approaching the current record weight of 5lb 9oz, taken by John Shayler from a private Kent lake. It is possible that these big fish are survivors from the ravages of the perch disease.

LOCATION AND FEEDING HABITS

The larger specimens are likely to be found and caught from the deeper areas of the water. With no weedbed cover they are likely to look for some cover in the form of sunken obstacles or depressions in the lake bed, from which they can ambush and strike at prey. In the deeper, darker water they find their prey by sensing the vibration of the small live fish or by smell. Ensure that you pierce the flesh of fresh deadbaits or fish half-baits to enhance their attraction.

METHODS

When it comes to catching perch there are certain times when particular methods are more practical. In the summer months the perch are most likely to be spread out evenly around the water and they can be caught on small spinners worked close to weedbeds and lily beds. Small brass Mepps spinners are likely to be the most successful.

Small and medium perch can be caught during the warmer months on maggot and worms. Figure 64 shows a simple float rig for presenting these baits. It can be a bit of a hit-and-miss affair but one thing is for sure: if you can get roach and rudd feeding there will always be the chance of attracting into the

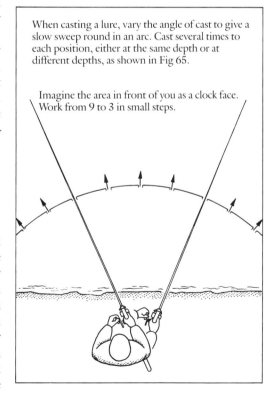

When casting a lure, vary the angle of cast to give a slow sweep round in an arc. Cast several times to each position, either at the same depth or at different depths, as shown in Fig 65.

Imagine the area in front of you as a clock face. Work from 9 to 3 in small steps.

Fig 63   Casting lures.

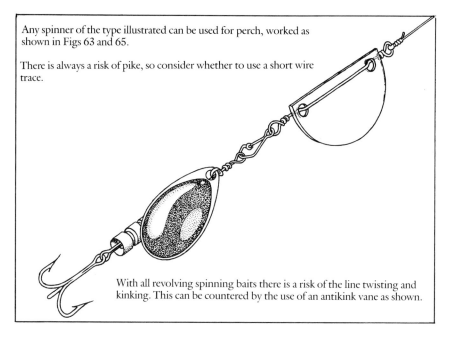

Any spinner of the type illustrated can be used for perch, worked as shown in Figs 63 and 65.

There is always a risk of pike, so consider whether to use a short wire trace.

With all revolving spinning baits there is a risk of the line twisting and kinking. This can be countered by the use of an antikink vane as shown.

Fig 64   Brass Mepps spinner with antikink vane.

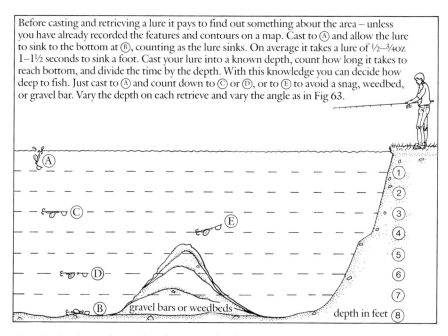

Before casting and retrieving a lure it pays to find out something about the area – unless you have already recorded the features and contours on a map. Cast to Ⓐ and allow the lure to sink to the bottom at Ⓑ, counting as the lure sinks. On average it takes a lure of ½–¾oz 1–1½ seconds to sink a foot. Cast your lure into a known depth, count how long it takes to reach bottom, and divide the time by the depth. With this knowledge you can decide how deep to fish. Just cast to Ⓐ and count down to Ⓒ or Ⓓ, or to Ⓔ to avoid a snag, weedbed, or gravel bar. Vary the depth on each retrieve and vary the angle as in Fig 63.

gravel bars or weedbeds

depth in feet

Fig 65   Casting and counting down to a depth.

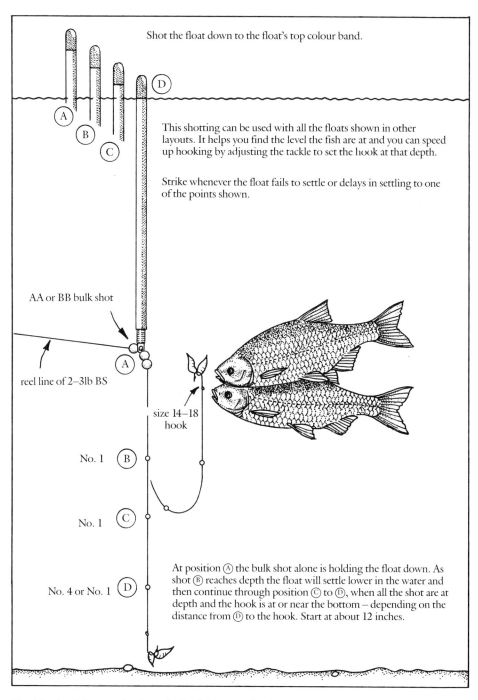

Shot the float down to the float's top colour band.

This shotting can be used with all the floats shown in other layouts. It helps you find the level the fish are at and you can speed up hooking by adjusting the tackle to set the hook at that depth.

Strike whenever the float fails to settle or delays in settling to one of the points shown.

AA or BB bulk shot

reel line of 2–3lb BS

size 14–18 hook

No. 1   B

No. 1   C

No. 4 or No. 1   D

At position Ⓐ the bulk shot alone is holding the float down. As shot Ⓑ reaches depth the float will settle lower in the water and then continue through position Ⓒ to Ⓓ, when all the shot are at depth and the hook is at or near the bottom – depending on the distance from Ⓓ to the hook. Start at about 12 inches.

Fig 66   Straight waggler float rig for fishing on the drop.

Keith Quantrell with a super perch of 2lb 14oz which took a 6oz roach intended as a pike bait.

The author with perch to 2lb 5oz taken on a small silver spoon jigged 12 inches off the bottom in 25 feet of water.

An early-season bag of perch to just over the 1lb mark for Mark Riley from a small town centre lake.

A 1lb 12oz specimen from a town lake for Wilf Crane.

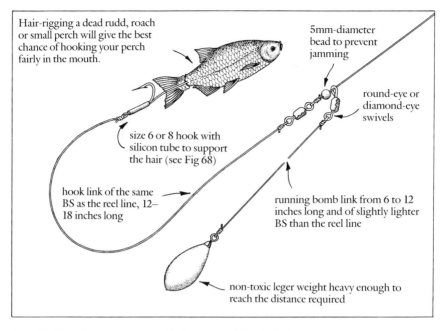

Hair-rigging a dead rudd, roach or small perch will give the best chance of hooking your perch fairly in the mouth.

5mm-diameter bead to prevent jamming

round-eye or diamond-eye swivels

size 6 or 8 hook with silicon tube to support the hair (see Fig 68)

hook link of the same BS as the reel line, 12–18 inches long

running bomb link from 6 to 12 inches long and of slightly lighter BS than the reel line

non-toxic leger weight heavy enough to reach the distance required

Fig 67   Running paternostered hair-mounted deadbait rig.

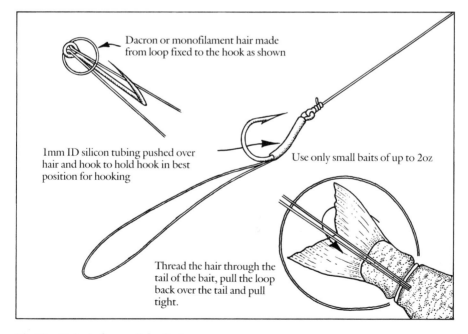

Dacron or monofilament hair made from loop fixed to the hook as shown

1mm ID silicon tubing pushed over hair and hook to hold hook in best position for hooking

Use only small baits of up to 2oz

Thread the hair through the tail of the bait, pull the loop back over the tail and pull tight.

Fig 68   Hair rig for small deadbaits.

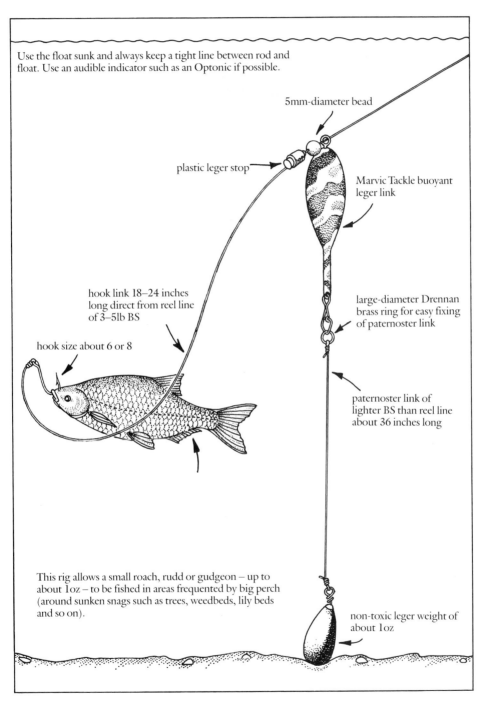

Use the float sunk and always keep a tight line between rod and float. Use an audible indicator such as an Optonic if possible.

5mm-diameter bead

plastic leger stop

Marvic Tackle buoyant leger link

hook link 18–24 inches long direct from reel line of 3–5lb BS

large-diameter Drennan brass ring for easy fixing of paternoster link

hook size about 6 or 8

paternoster link of lighter BS than reel line about 36 inches long

This rig allows a small roach, rudd or gudgeon – up to about 1oz – to be fished in areas frequented by big perch (around sunken snags such as trees, weedbeds, lily beds and so on).

non-toxic leger weight of about 1oz

Fig 69   Float-paternostered livebait rig (sunk).

Barbara Hancock displays a super perch of 1lb 8oz taken from her local town centre lake.

swim either a shoal of perch or perhaps a bigger specimen or two. Continual loose feeding with maggot can help build up a swim.

If a bigger, specimen-size perch is your goal you will need to wait until the autumn and winter to stand any real chance of success. At this time those solitary bigger perch tend to move to deeper sections of the water and become part of a shoal. Location is now the most important factor. If you have noted the deeper channels or depressions on the lake you can begin your search there.

Your choice of methods here will be legered deadbaits, lobworms, or paternostered small livebaits, such as minnows, gudgeon or small roach. Figure 67 shows a basic leger rig which can be used with either worms or deadbaits. If you wish to use deadbaits, remember that your bait is likely to be taken head first and usually swallowed quickly once the perch is sure it is safe to do so. Badly mounted baits can result in deep hooking with sure loss of life if the perch is badly handled.

Figure 68 shows how to hair-rig deadbait to avoid deep hooking. The method also aids hooking, in that the hook is not masked by the bait. If you fail to hook your perch on getting a take, it may be because the perch sensed some resistance and decided to drop the bait anyway. A better way of fishing deadbaits is to use the bait and just a small amount of shot to hold it down and aid casting. A small float can also be used fished overdepth by a couple of feet. If you choose to fish with simple leger, after casting tighten up to the bait and use a small bobbin like that illustrated in Figure 34 in conjunction with an Optonic indicator if you own one.

If you are fishing at extreme range with a full leger rig, use one like the one illustrated in Figure 67. Use a similar indicator, once again in conjunction with an Optonic – or with a long drop below the rod – to give plenty of visual indication and time for the perch to gain confidence. Always fish with the bail arm *open*.

The final and often most effective method of catching perch once they have shoaled up in their winter haunt is with small livebaits paternostered a few feet off the bottom. Figure 69 shows how to set this rig up. With this method, of course, you will have to catch or obtain a good supply of healthy livebaits, usually before you start fishing. The size of bait is not too restrictive. Smaller baits are usually around an ounce in weight with a suitable maximum of 2oz, though a big perch may take a roach of up to 8oz. The perch shown in the photograph at the top of page 78 weighed in at 2lb 14oz and was taken by Keith Quantrill on a 6oz roach.

Keep a reasonably tight line from the rod tip to the float, which is fished sunken. Ensure that the bail arm is open and be prepared for sizzling runs.

You may well fish for perch at depths of up to 30 feet and more. If so, you must consider the effect of bringing a fish up from such deep water. Please be careful. When fishing at depths of over 20 feet, play your fish up to the surface *slowly* and in stages, giving the perch time to adjust to the change in pressure. Rush the fish to the surface and you will witness the swim bladder blowing up and popping out of the perch's throat, which will kill the fish. Even cautiously raised fish get into difficulty with inflated swim bladders. Take great care with all your perch, particularly in the way you hook your baits, and we can all enjoy having a go at catching good fish.

7 Roach (Rutilus rutilus)

Whilst fewer stillwaters seem to have large quantities of very easy-to-catch small rudd and perch, it would be very hard to find a still-water that does not have a large population of small roach. Of all the species the roach is the one with the ability to reproduce and survive in large numbers – to the point where it can affect the balance and growth of both itself and other resident species. Remember that a water can only support a given weight of fish per acre. Many of our unmanaged small fisheries eventually end up in this sort of state – a large head of small to medium-size roach and, if you are lucky, a few big roach. Occasionally you will be lucky enough to find a water which contains a good head of big roach – probably one of the bigger gravel pits or reservoirs, which may well have a good population of predators such as perch and

pike to consume the roach fry and cut down the larger year classes.

IDENTIFICATION

In its early years the young roach is bright silver in colour and is long and slender. This changes as the roach matures. It grows deep in the body and takes on a dark green-bronze hue on the back with a lighter shade of bronze appearing down its flanks. In healthy, vibrant, mature examples of this species a distinct blue sheen can be seen on the back and flanks in sunlight.

The head is fairly small. The eyes have bright-red irises, and this colour in various hues is mirrored in the fins, which run from orange to bright red. The mouth is fairly small and there are no barbels.

The pelvic fins have from 9 to 11 branched rays. The short-based dorsal fin originates directly above the base of the pelvic fins. The lateral line has from 42 to 45 scales.

SPAWNING HABITS

The prolific nature of the roach results from its ability to tolerate both high and low temperatures and oxygen levels and the fact that it reaches sexual maturity at the relatively young age of 2 or 3 years. Each female is capable of producing between 1,000 and 15,000 eggs,

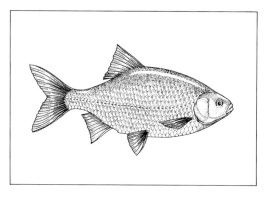

Fig 70   The roach, *Rutilus rutilus*.

depending on individual size. Spawning takes place from about April through to June, depending on water temperature. The eggs hatch in 9–12 days with a water temperature of between 12 and 14 degrees centigrade. The small larvae remain in the weed for a day or so longer before becoming mobile and forming large schools and moving into the warm shallow marginal areas of water.

At this stage in life the fry feed on small diatoms and crustaceans eventually moving on as they grow to feed on whatever food source is most prolific – insect larvae, crustaceans, worms, and so on. Growth rate depends on food supply and competition. Given the right combination of low numbers and an abundance of food, roach can live to an age of 12 years or so and grow to the

weight of the record fish of 4lb 1oz caught from a Nottinghamshire gravel pit in 1975 by Richard Jones.

LOCATION AND FEEDING HABITS

The feeding habits of the mature fish do not differ much from the infant diet, except in quantity. Adult roach learn by searching where to find seasonal abundance in the form of bloodworms, snails, or whatever. Between feeding spells roach are a patrolling, roving species, and this is how they find new sources of food. If we could identify the feeding sites finding the roach would be simple. All we can do is look for the areas they are likely to fre-

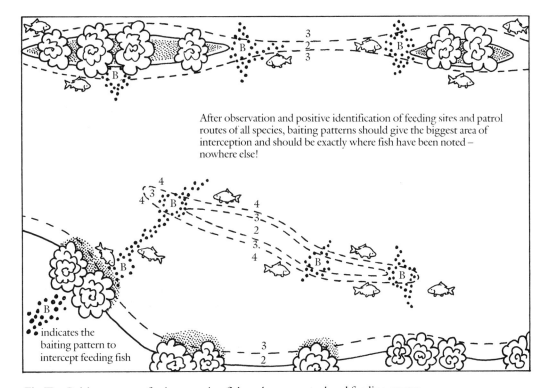

Fig 71   Baiting patterns for intercepting fish on known patrol and feeding routes.

The author fishes with a tube bobbin to slow down the bites which had been lightning-fast and unhittable on the quivertip.

The author takes time to admire a super roach taken on maggot from Clumber Park Lake on swimfeeder tactics.

The author supports the sort of fish that can be expected if the choice of venue, location, tactics and bait are all correct.

Jim Bigden admires a nice roach in the glow of the setting sun at Weirwood Reservoir.

quent – gravel bars, plateaux, and the like. They are not often found in and around lily beds, weedbeds or reedbeds, preferring cleaner gravelly areas and open water.

WEATHER AND SEASONAL EFFECTS

A fish for all seasons, maybe! You will find that roach will be the first to bite whenever you fish, from early summer through to early spring. The important thing is the weather. Whilst warm summery weather will see the shoals of small fish active, the better sizes of fish are active during the autumn and winter months.

Whilst roach will feed in the depths of winter it is during milder, wetter periods that some better returns can be expected, particularly if there is colour in the water and wind

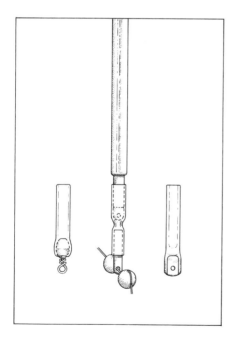

Fig 72   Various float adaptors.

and cloud to roughen the water and keep light levels down. Bites often seem to pick up in late afternoon on the brighter days. In summer you may get better returns of quality fish during overcast periods with rain, and particularly at dusk and overnight. Light levels play an important part in roach behaviour.

METHODS

It is doubtful whether any method – apart from pike-fishing methods – will *not* catch roach. Certainly, at some time or another they take just about every bait you might put out for any of the other species.

Laying On

A typical method of catching roach is laying on with float tackle. It is nothing super-sophisticated but a practical method which presents the bait where roach appear to like it, on the bottom. The type of bottom does have some bearing on success; soft silty bottoms require light, buoyant baits, such as crust or bread flake, lightly pinched on to the hook; baits such as maggots and corn are better over a clean bottom, of which gravel pits provide the best example.

Figure 73 illustrates a float rig layout fished in conjunction with a suitable bait over a bed of groundbait in the form suited to the water – breadcrumb or mashed bread mixed with hookbait samples over silt, or loose feed of sweetcorn or maggots introduced at regular intervals over a hard bottom. Hemp in its various forms can prove a powerful attractor to roach during the summer months and tares can be used as hookbait.

The rig is best fished slightly overdepth with a good length of line actually on the bottom, though this can be varied to improve

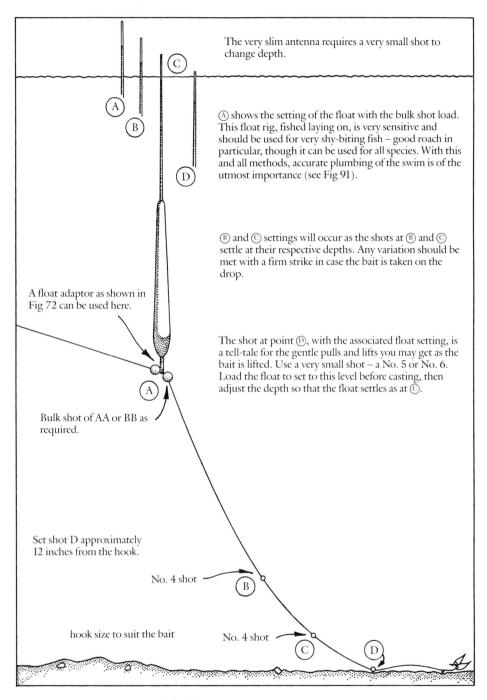

The very slim antenna requires a very small shot to change depth.

(A) shows the setting of the float with the bulk shot load. This float rig, fished laying on, is very sensitive and should be used for very shy-biting fish – good roach in particular, though it can be used for all species. With this and all methods, accurate plumbing of the swim is of the utmost importance (see Fig 91).

(B) and (C) settings will occur as the shots at (B) and (C) settle at their respective depths. Any variation should be met with a firm strike in case the bait is taken on the drop.

A float adaptor as shown in Fig 72 can be used here.

The shot at point (D), with the associated float setting, is a tell-tale for the gentle pulls and lifts you may get as the bait is lifted. Use a very small shot – a No. 5 or No. 6. Load the float to set to this level before casting, then adjust the depth so that the float settles as at (C).

Bulk shot of AA or BB as required.

Set shot D approximately 12 inches from the hook.

No. 4 shot

hook size to suit the bait

No. 4 shot

Fig 73   Stillwater blue set to fish laying on.

Chris Turnbull plays a nice roach to the net, taken at long range on swimfeedered maggot.

bite indication. Bites will usually see the float slowly moving away as the bait is taken. Sometimes it pays to wait and see if the bite develops. If the roach are confident and of good size they will usually take the bait slowly and continue. If you leave lightning-fast bites alone you will likely find that the float re-appears a second later. These bites are from small fish.

Swimfeeder Fishing

Just as successful as float fishing is swimfeeder fishing. Figure 74 shows the basic set-up which will allow you to offer a variety of baits. Swimfeeder methods described in other chapters can be used to achieve similar results with different baits. The feeder illustrated is the Drennan feeder link and, whilst its main purpose was to feed maggots, it can be modified as shown in Figure 75 to take any other bait held in by a plug of groundbait mixed to

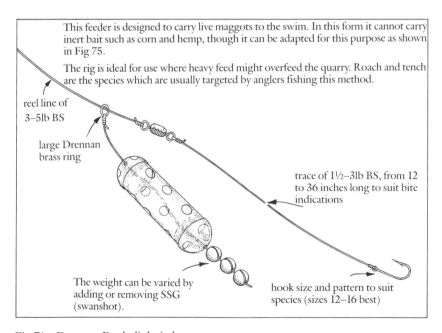

This feeder is designed to carry live maggots to the swim. In this form it cannot carry inert bait such as corn and hemp, though it can be adapted for this purpose as shown in Fig 75.

The rig is ideal for use where heavy feed might overfeed the quarry. Roach and tench are the species which are usually targeted by anglers fishing this method.

reel line of 3–5lb BS

large Drennan brass ring

trace of 1½–3lb BS, from 12 to 36 inches long to suit bite indications

The weight can be varied by adding or removing SSG (swanshot).

hook size and pattern to suit species (sizes 12–16 best)

Fig 74   Drennan Feederlink rig layout.

dry texture. The dry plug expands as it takes up water and falls out of the feeder. It is also possible to use just a filling of groundbait, provided it is not pushed in too firmly.

Feeder fishing allows you to place groundbait and hookbait accurately, it is important to achieve accuracy with each cast so that you are fishing as often as possible in exactly the same spot. If you cast to different areas you will split the fish up and reduce the opportunity of catching a good bag. Chapter 10 describes ways of ensuring accurate castings.

When you start feeder fishing begin by casting several loaded feeders into the swim in quick succession to build up a base of attractor which you will continue to build up slowly with each future cast. A good mix of hemp, corn or maggots with a plug of groundbait will usually attract roach. The most important ingredients are hemp and maggots. Whichever bait you choose for the hook should be included in small quantities in the

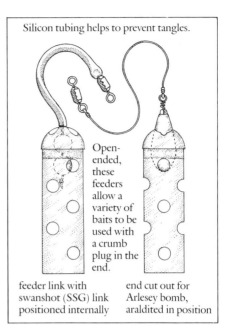

Silicon tubing helps to prevent tangles.

Open-ended, these feeders allow a variety of baits to be used with a crumb plug in the end.

feeder link with swanshot (SSG) link positioned internally

end cut out for Arlesey bomb, araldited in position

Fig 75   Modified Drennan feeder links.

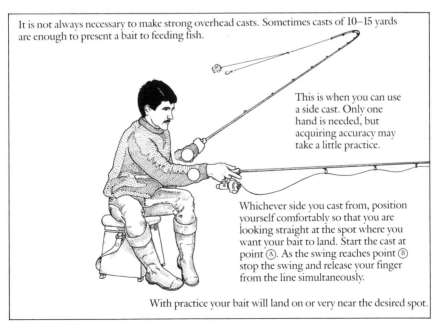

It is not always necessary to make strong overhead casts. Sometimes casts of 10–15 yards are enough to present a bait to feeding fish.

This is when you can use a side cast. Only one hand is needed, but acquiring accuracy may take a little practice.

Whichever side you cast from, position yourself comfortably so that you are looking straight at the spot where you want your bait to land. Start the cast at point Ⓐ. As the swing reaches point Ⓑ stop the swing and release your finger from the line simultaneously.

With practice your bait will land on or very near the desired spot.

Fig 76   Side casting with one hand.

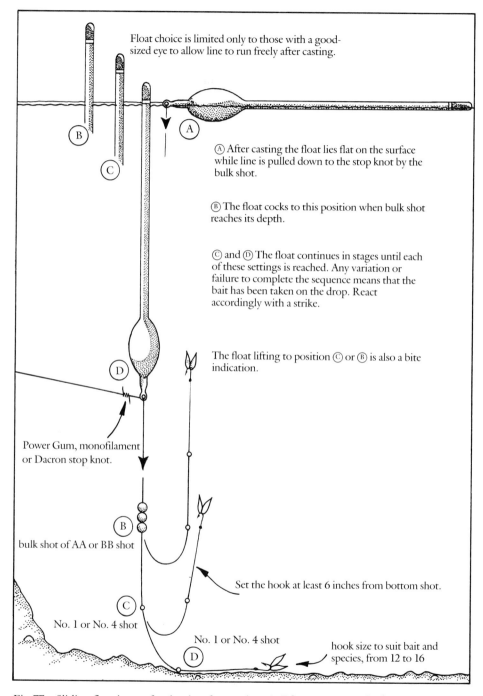

Float choice is limited only to those with a good-sized eye to allow line to run freely after casting.

B

C

A

Ⓐ After casting the float lies flat on the surface while line is pulled down to the stop knot by the bulk shot.

Ⓑ The float cocks to this position when bulk shot reaches its depth.

Ⓒ and Ⓓ The float continues in stages until each of these settings is reached. Any variation or failure to complete the sequence means that the bait has been taken on the drop. React accordingly with a strike.

D

The float lifting to position Ⓒ or Ⓑ is also a bite indication.

Power Gum, monofilament or Dacron stop knot.

B

bulk shot of AA or BB shot

Set the hook at least 6 inches from bottom shot.

C

No. 1 or No. 4 shot

No. 1 or No. 4 shot

D

hook size to suit bait and species, from 12 to 16

Fig 77   Sliding float layout for depths of more than 6–7 feet – or as required.

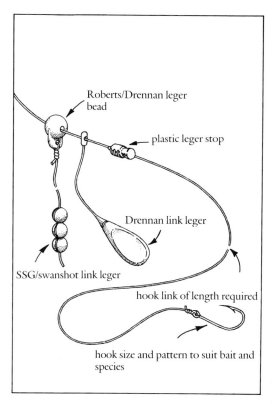

Roberts/Drennan leger
bead

plastic leger stop

Drennan link leger

SSG/swanshot link leger

hook link of length required

hook size and pattern to suit bait and
species

Fig 78   Assorted leger links.

feeder. Bite indication can be by swingtip, quivertip or butt indicators, as shown in Figure 36. Small light bobbins can also be used, as can butt and bobbin indicators in conjunction with an Optonic indicator.

The tail lengths of the hook and the feeder must be adjusted to suit the swim and feeding habits. Weed may influence this; gravel does too. Try to avoid weedbeds, but if you have to fish near them then use a long tail to prevent the hookbait becoming obscured. The early season will see the roach taking fairly boldly, so you will find that a tail length of between 18 and 24 inches will serve well, although it will pay to start at about 12 inches with the feeder either directly on the line or with a short link of 4–6 inches. As the fish get more cautious it may pay to extend the hook link to lengths as long as 5 feet. That is an extreme but it may help produce extra roach when they are difficult. Feeder links can remain short or they can be adjusted in length to balance the rig. Do not be afraid to try the two extremes of very short or very long hook links if the bites stop coming. The slightest adjustment may get a response.

8 Rudd (Scardinius erythrophthalmus)

Like small perch, rudd are amongst most new anglers' early successes, though this success is due in many cases to the anglers' lack of experience. Where rudd are found in large numbers they invariably form large year-class shoals which can be found on most sunny days frequenting the warm upper surface layers of the water. It is with these shoals of rudd that the lucky angler who has unknowingly set up his tackle incorrectly finds his or her inexplicable success. It is likely that the tackle is either fished too shallow or is badly shotted and effectively provides the angler with a rig that fishes the bait 'on the drop' – not that the angler realises this fact! Also, the majority of these early captures of rudd are limited to small fish of just a few ounces, and it is common for the angler to mistakenly identify his catch as a roach since the two

species look so uncannily alike in their early years.

IDENTIFICATION

Close inspection of the rudd reveals some very distinctive characteristics, which, if remembered, will help you instantly recognise any future captures. Of all the features the mouth is the most significant. Unlike the mouths of other cyprinid species it slopes upwards, with the lower jaw on smaller fish coming up level with the red-ringed eyes. The rudd takes its specific name from a Greek word meaning 'red eyes'.

The body of an adult rudd is deep with a dark greeny-bronze hue to the back. The flanks are much brighter, almost golden in colour, and this is accentuated by the high dorsal fin with its 8 or 9 branched rays – which, unlike the roach, is well behind the line of the pelvic fins – and the anal fin with its long base and 10 or 11 branched rays. Both the pelvic and the anal fins are scarlet-coloured, whilst the remaining fins and tail are tinted a lighter shade of red.

SPAWNING HABITS

Spawning takes place between April and June, depending on weather conditions and water temperatures. Each female rudd can

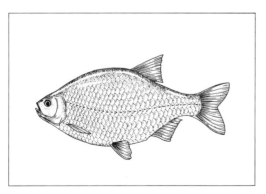

Fig 79   The rudd, *Scardinius erythrophthalmus*.

The beauty of a superb golden-bronze rudd is admired by its captor, John Wilson.

Many anglers' first capture, a surface-caught rudd for a young Lee Wilson.

The unmistakable golden hue of a beautiful rudd.

produce between 90,000 and 200,000 eggs, depending on the fish's size. The eggs are usually laid in reedbeds and on water plants and will, depending on water temperature again, hatch in about 8–15 days.

With the prolific spawning potential of the rudd it is infrequent that fish grow to more than about 1–1½lb. This is because of the demand on the food supply. Only if few rudd are present in the water are they likely to grow into potential record breakers. Many rudd waters become overrun with thousands of rudd which may only weigh between 2 and 6oz. An example of the potential for rudd to grow to specimen and record-making size is the current record rudd, which weighed 4lb 8oz and was caught by the late Revd. E. C. Alston in 1933 from Ringmere near Thetford

in Norfolk. The reason why Ringmere was able to produce such a huge fish – and it did produce others – is that the stock of rudd was introduced by the Revd. Alston from a catch of fish he had taken a few years earlier from Stanford Water, a couple of miles away. The few introduced rudd were able to feed and grow without restriction. Alas, Ringmere was to do what it does every decade or so, dry up, which eliminated the chance of repeating the Revd. Alston's feat.

LOCATION AND FEEDING HABITS

After hatching the fry eat insect larvae. As they mature this diet is supplemented by additional food sources such as small molluscs, shrimps and algae, which may contain other food items. A great deal of the rudd's feeding takes place at or near the surface, on the underside of lilies, the stems of reeds and other water plants, and on any insect hatches that take place throughout the season.

Very often rudd can be seen in large shoals just under the surface, particularly on warm bright days. On days like this surface or slow-sinking baits may be taken quite readily! Surface shoals are very easy to locate since they are very easily startled by bankside activity or the sight of a bird flying overhead. The shoals tend to scatter in a rather splashy eruption and reform a few moments later.

Whilst rudd shoals can be seen anywhere and at any time on the lake or pit, more often than not they are close to a feature such as a lily bed, a reedbed or a fallen tree. The larger specimens are more likely to exhibit this sort of behaviour and may be found well away from popular areas, seeking both areas of sanctuary and abundant food supply.

WEATHER AND SEASONAL EFFECTS

Like many species today the humble rudd ranks low in the order of popularity and is normally associated with summer since it is highly visible at that time of year, with its liking for the warm surface layers and the seasonal insect hatches and larvae. As a result,

most of those anglers who seek to catch rudd by design do so during the summer months; very few bother during the cooler months of November through to March. To confirm that they can be caught during the winter, talk to a keen pike angler who has tried to catch roach for livebaits. Rudd are usually more than willing to feed on all but the coldest days of winter.

Winter rudd will invariably take a bottom-fished bait, maggot being the most popular. Like most species, rudd respond to wind direction, and for the same reasons – marginal disturbance and the associated release of food items from the bank and reedbeds and other plants.

METHODS

The secret of catching rudd, particularly the bigger specimens, comes from understanding their habits, likes and dislikes and then actually locating them at the chosen venue. If you can track down your target there is every chance of catching them on any of the float and leger methods described in the chapters on the other species.

Some methods, however, both float and leger, are a little more selective for catching rudd. The method shown in Figure 80 is not the normal style of float fishing you will be familiar with. Float fishing for rudd can be the most frustrating of methods as the bites demand that you are alert and quick to react; when they come they are usually lightning-fast. The float rig illustrated is very useful if the rudd are at close range, possibly over the edge of a weed-bed or lily bed, and where casting is not of any great importance and you can get away with little or no shot on the line. The most important point with this float rig is that the line must be lightly greased with a small amount of silicon Mucilin to make it

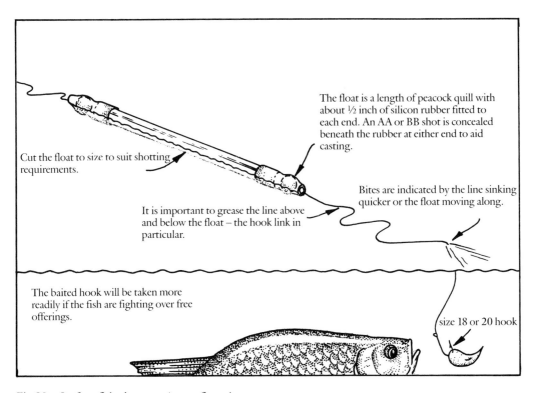

The float is a length of peacock quill with about ½ inch of silicon rubber fitted to each end. An AA or BB shot is concealed beneath the rubber at either end to aid casting.

Cut the float to size to suit shotting requirements.

Bites are indicated by the line sinking quicker or the float moving along.

It is important to grease the line above and below the float – the hook link in particular.

The baited hook will be taken more readily if the fish are fighting over free offerings.

size 18 or 20 hook

Fig 80   Surface-fished maggot/caster float rig.

float and just allow the baited hook, if it is baited with a buoyant maggot, to sink very, very slowly.

Bites are indicated by the line sinking much quicker than normal or by the line and float moving across the surface before disappearing. Whichever sign you get, strike fast. You should always hold the rod when fishing this method and pay close attention to the float if you wish to have any good rudd gracing your landing net. It is no use putting the rod in the rodrest as all but the smallest fish will eject the bait and hook before you can lift the rod.

It can be very effective to keep the line from rod tip to float as tight as possible and period-ically recover some line, thereby twitching the bait along, if no bites are forthcoming, to tempt a response from the rudd. The regular

introduction of loose feed in the form of just a few maggots to keep the rudd active will soon see you catching fish. Cast your baited rig into or just beyond the fish just after throwing or catapulting in some maggots and be ready to strike!

If the rudd are out of range of the method just described the rig shown in Figure 81 can be effective. It is a waggler float with all the shot accumulated directly at the base of the float. This allows easy casting to the feeding area while maintaining the advantage of a slow-sinking bait. If you use the same tactic of catapulting a few maggots out to the rudd before the cast, it should entice an almost instant bite. Remember to hold the rod and be ready for a quick strike! Hook-link length can be as long as you wish. Start with at least

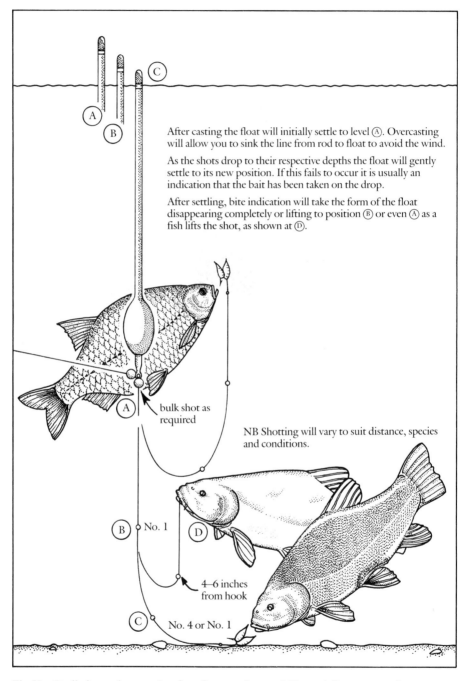

After casting the float will initially settle to level Ⓐ. Overcasting will allow you to sink the line from rod to float to avoid the wind.

As the shots drop to their respective depths the float will gently settle to its new position. If this fails to occur it is usually an indication that the bait has been taken on the drop.

After settling, bite indication will take the form of the float disappearing completely or lifting to position Ⓑ or even Ⓐ as a fish lifts the shot, as shown at Ⓓ.

bulk shot as required

NB Shotting will vary to suit distance, species and conditions.

Ⓑ No. 1

4–6 inches from hook

Ⓒ No. 4 or No. 1

Fig 81   Bodied waggler or onion float for use where stability and distance are of prime importance.

John Wilson plays a good rudd on an Irish lough.

36 inches, see how the bites develop, and shorten or lengthen as you feel necessary.

As the season develops and the bigger rudd move out to safer areas – perhaps beyond range for good float fishing – you may have to turn to leger fishing to present them with a bait. Figure 84 illustrates a good rig for presenting a floating or slow-sinking bait at the required distance. Probably the most important thing is knowing how deep the water is at the point where the rudd are active so that you can adjust the tail length to allow good bait presentation, particularly if you are fishing a surface bait.

This may require a few trial casts to get it right. It would be wise to note the area the fish like and try to plumb the depth there when the rudd are not in residence, as frequent casting will only hasten their moving to

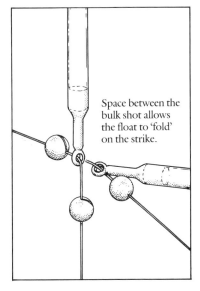

Space between the bulk shot allows the float to 'fold' on the strike.

Fig 82   Waggler locking-shot layout.

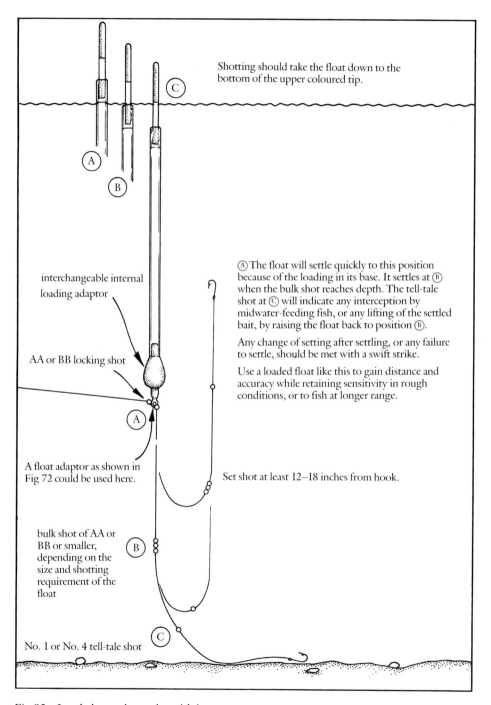

Shotting should take the float down to the bottom of the upper coloured tip.

interchangeable internal loading adaptor

AA or BB locking shot

Ⓐ The float will settle quickly to this position because of the loading in its base. It settles at Ⓑ when the bulk shot reaches depth. The tell-tale shot at Ⓒ will indicate any interception by midwater-feeding fish, or any lifting of the settled bait, by raising the float back to position Ⓑ.

Any change of setting after settling, or any failure to settle, should be met with a swift strike.

Use a loaded float like this to gain distance and accuracy while retaining sensitivity in rough conditions, or to fish at longer range.

A float adaptor as shown in Fig 72 could be used here.

Set shot at least 12–18 inches from hook.

bulk shot of AA or BB or smaller, depending on the size and shotting requirement of the float

No. 1 or No. 4 tell-tale shot

Fig 83   Loaded crystal waggler with insert.

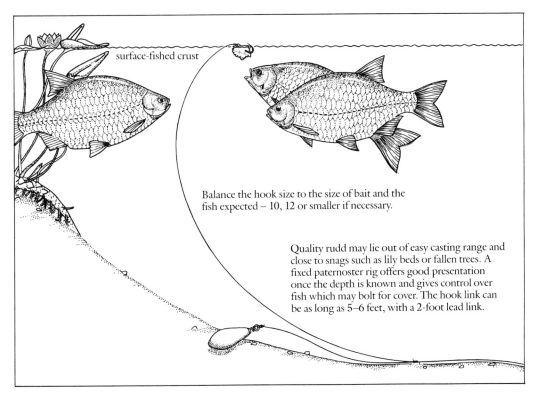

surface-fished crust

Balance the hook size to the size of bait and the
fish expected – 10, 12 or smaller if necessary.

Quality rudd may lie out of easy casting range and
close to snags such as lily beds or fallen trees. A
fixed paternoster rig offers good presentation
once the depth is known and gives control over
fish which may bolt for cover. The hook link can
be as long as 5–6 feet, with a 2-foot lead link.

Fig 84   Surface-fished crust on a fixed paternoster.

a new safe area and you will have to start all over again.

All the usual baits can be used – maggots, worm, and so on – but bread flake and a small piece of crust are superb, both for slow-sinking and floating baits. The rig illustrated is a fixed paternoster, but you could equally use a running paternoster rig. Reel line should be about 5lb to deal with casting. The hook link can be from 2 to 5lb, depending on how great a risk snags present.

Hooks should be matched both in size and pattern to the swim and the line, sizes 10–12 for flake and crust, 14–16 for maggot or small red worms.

Bite indication is vital, and the combination of small bobbin and Optonic can be very successful, as can quivertipping and butt indicators. The important thing with any method is to stay close to your rods, keep alert to spot a bite developing, and strike at the right moment to set the hook.

9 Tench (Tinca tinca)

Tench are the early-season species, tradition-ally the one species many anglers set out to catch on the opening morning of the new season. There is something special about fish-ing for tench on float tackle at dawn when the water is flat calm, with the masses of small bubbles appearing with increasing frequency and quantity around your float.

The lifting and laying flat of the float is the prelude to a spectacular battle – which is explained once the fish is landed. The power comes from the large shovel-like tail and the large pelvic fins. In the male the size and shape of these pelvic fins are particularly noticeable. They are larger than those of the female and there is a pronounced ridge immediately above them. Another noticeable feature in the male is that it never attains the size of the female. Usually in a given water there may be a weight difference of as much as 3lb between them. If you are lucky enough to catch a good-size male tench of more than

5lb, you might be lucky enough to be fishing a water that holds tench of over 7lb.

IDENTIFICATION

The tench's fins are fully rounded in shape and, when erect, they give a very balanced look to the sleek shape of the fish. The dorsal fin is made up of 10 or 11 branched rays and the anal fin of 8–10 branched rays. Unlike many of the other cyprinid species where the scales are large and coarse, the scales on the tench are very small and deeply embedded. They are also covered in a thick mucous coat-ing. These two features combine to make the tench easily identifiable, even in the dark. One touch and you will instinctively know that you have caught your tench. The colour of the tench is invariably a deep olive-green, but it does vary according to environment. Some fish from dark, peaty waters can look almost black whilst some from gravel pits take on an almost golden glow, looking almost like the very rare golden-yellow tench.

The head of the tench is also very distinc-tive with its bold 'teddy-bear' eyes of yellow and red, and the single barbel on either side of its large semi-extendable mouth, which it uses for rooting around in the bottom debris for food items. It is this activity that creates all those telltale bubbles. As the tench takes in food it also takes in debris and bottom gases, which pass through its gill rakers and are expelled to produce the masses of tiny pinhead-sized bubbles that fizz on the surface

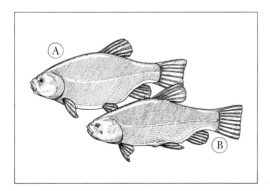

Fig 85　The tench, *Tinca tinca* (Ⓑ female, Ⓐ male).

– all the more exciting if this happens over your groundbait and beside your float. It really gets the adrenalin surging.

A rather elusive fish, the tench can prove very difficult to catch in some lakes. They tend to stay tight inside the confines of weedy areas and those that are hooked prove very difficult to extract. While tench may be easy to catch in waters where shoals of smaller, younger fish predominate, on waters which will produce fish of specimen proportions, they are hard to tempt.

SPAWNING HABITS

In general terms there are no stillwaters which will not support tench as a species but some kinds of water do offer more of what tench need to both grow and reproduce in sufficient quantities to make a good tench fishery.

If the water is of the right quality, is exposed to sunlight and wind, and has a good growth of weed, there is every chance that spawning will take place at some time between late May and early July, depending really on high enough water temperature. In many waters the tench are still carrying spawn and subsequently a lot of extra weight in the opening weeks of the season. Since a female tench can carry between 300,000 and 900,000 eggs the extra weight can be considerable. For this reason it is important to handle early season tench with extreme care and not cram them into keepnets. If successful spawning takes place the eggs hatch in 6–8 days, depending on water temperature. For about ten days the larvae live off the yolk of the egg. Then they become self-supporting, at first eating insect larvae and then food items of increasing size as they grow. On waters with plenty of cover the small tench become very elusive as they grow and though small tench may be present in good numbers they are very seldom

caught. It is very rare to catch tench under ½ or ¾lb except in small overstocked waters.

LOCATION AND FEEDING HABITS

All of the information above should help in the understanding of the habits of tench and thus in their location. Notes given in Chapter 5 on the location of carp can also be applied to tench. You need to find areas which are likely to hold the sort of food items that tench like – bloodworms, snails and crustaceans. Such areas are usually in and around the water plants, weedbeds and reedbeds, and feeding

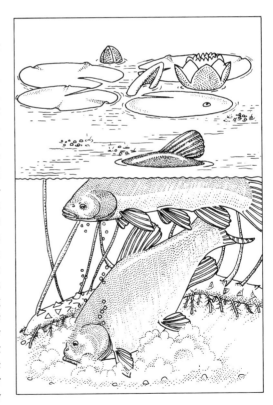

Fig 86 Tench bubbling and rolling in their feeding area.

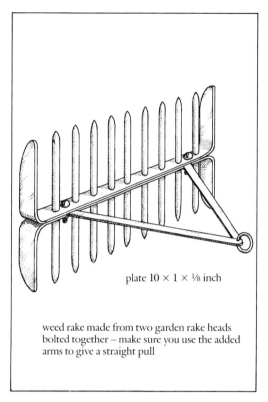

plate 10 × 1 × ⅛ inch

weed rake made from two garden rake heads
bolted together – make sure you use the added
arms to give a straight pull

Fig 87   Typical weed rake.

tench actually consume a considerable amount of vegetable matter. Once you have found areas worthy of attention there is no substitute for sitting and watching to identify whether the swim actually holds or is visited by *feeding* tench.

Depending on water clarity you may or may not be able actually to see the tench, but when they are there and feeding you will most certainly see two typical signs: the most obvious of these is the appearance of patches of small bubbles fizzing up to the surface. If tench are the cause it will soon be confirmed by the second indication: rolling on the surface. It is difficult to describe but takes the form of slow, splashless rolls, which you will recognise when they occur.

Other favourite areas are shallow gravel bars covered in weed or reeds, which may support a good population of snails and crustaceans. It can pay to avoid large areas of open water. Tench just do not seem to like open water but definitely prefer cover – probably a legacy from their nursery days when they spend so much time in weedbeds. An exception to this rule is when the bottom is raked, causing the silt to rise in suspension, along with many tiny food items, while larger items, normally concealed, are released to the surface. The tench is very sensitive to the smell of food and will forsake sanctuary to make the most of free natural food, but only if there is some form of cover, such as the cloudy water caused by the raking. Try this if you have to fish in open water or alongside reedbeds and cannot draw fish to your groundbait and free offerings.

WEATHER AND SEASONAL EFFECTS

It is very difficult to say how weather and the seasons affect the habits of tench. The tench has always been considered a typical summer species, perhaps hibernating from the end of September. That was also the theory on carp until a few dedicated carp anglers in the late 1960s decided to try to catch carp in winter. The results are well known. Now winter carping is almost as popular and successful as summer carping. So what of tench? There are certainly considerable numbers of *chance* captures in January, February and March, which tends to indicate that tench are active and do not hibernate. Perhaps tench are simply neglected in winter as anglers follow tradition and turn their attention to such winter species as pike, chub, roach and perch.

Wind, rain and sunshine are the important

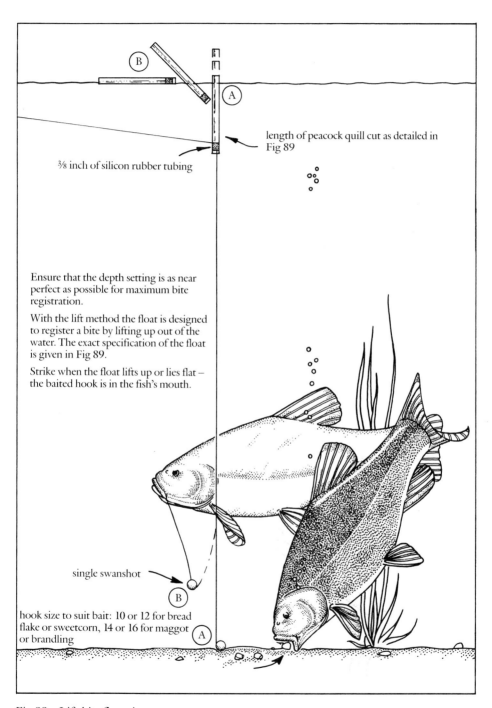

B

A

length of peacock quill cut as detailed in Fig 89

³⁄₈ inch of silicon rubber tubing

Ensure that the depth setting is as near perfect as possible for maximum bite registration.

With the lift method the float is designed to register a bite by lifting up out of the water. The exact specification of the float is given in Fig 89.

Strike when the float lifts up or lies flat – the baited hook is in the fish's mouth.

single swanshot

B

hook size to suit bait: 10 or 12 for bread flake or sweetcorn, 14 or 16 for maggot or brandling

A

Fig 88   Lift-bite float rig.

elements in tench fishing. Each can affect the feeding habits of tench enough to turn them on or off. Wind can cool the water, turning the fish off feed. Too much bright sun can raise the temperature of the water with the same effect, making tench feed for short periods early in the morning.

Wind probably has the greatest influence on when and where tench feed, and this phenomenon is common to many other species as well. The bank which has received the prevailing wind for several days benefits from bankside wave agitation which releases and stirs up food items which are distributed by the undertow for some distance over the lake or pit bottom. The water may even become well coloured, which further encourages attention of tench. Make a note of wind

direction and at least check the downwind areas for signs of feeding. It is no use fishing for tench in areas where they do not feed or which they do not visit willingly. Observation does pay dividends!

METHODS

Many of the methods described in the other chapters can be used to catch tench, provided you are fishing where tench feed.

Probably the one method that automatically comes to the mind of any traditional tench angler is the so-called 'lift method' of float fishing. In many situations this is a very practical and most enjoyable method of catching tench. Figures 89 and 90 show how to set

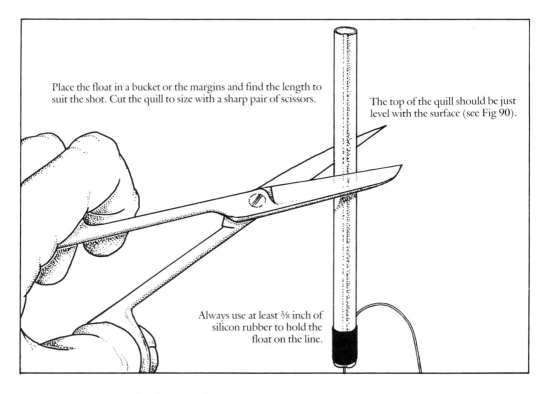

Place the float in a bucket or the margins and find the length to suit the shot. Cut the quill to size with a sharp pair of scissors.

The top of the quill should be just level with the surface (see Fig 90).

Always use at least ⅜ inch of silicon rubber to hold the float on the line.

Fig 89   Cutting peacock quill to match shotting.

The profiles of the male and female tench are unmistakable. The upper fish is the male, the lower the female.

A nice brace of opening-morning tench from a bag taken on float-fished bread flake from a small estate lake.

The author with a nice catch of tench to just over 4lb, the result of weed clearance and raking prior to fishing.

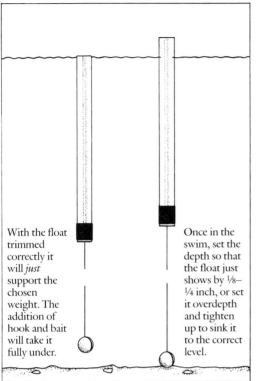

With the float trimmed correctly it will *just* support the chosen weight. The addition of hook and bait will take it fully under.

Once in the swim, set the depth so that the float just shows by 1/8–1/4 inch, or set it overdepth and tighten up to sink it to the correct level.

Fig 90   Setting the depth of float and shot.

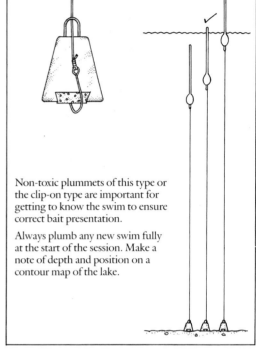

Non-toxic plummets of this type or the clip-on type are important for getting to know the swim to ensure correct bait presentation.

Always plumb any new swim fully at the start of the session. Make a note of depth and position on a contour map of the lake.

Fig 91   Using a plummet.

up a traditional rig and how to get the float to size.

If you locate an early-season tench feeding area, raking or prebaiting the evening before a dawn fishing session will maximise your chance of catching. You can also plumb the depth of your swim to save wasting time in the poor light of dawn. Once you arrive and get tackled up, introduce a small amount of free hook samples – sweetcorn, maggots or bread flake – to top up the previous free offerings and then cast into position with the baited rig. Do not rush in and pound the swim with too much groundbait, as this may spook and frighten the tench. Far better to wait and eventually introduce small amounts of mashed bread or crumbs to the swim.

With the rig illustrated in Figure 88, if you have taken the time to get the float and shot balance right then as soon as the tench picks up the baited hook the float will also lift and may actually lie flat before slowly disappearing fully as the fish moves off. As soon as the float lifts well and stays up, strike to set the hook. Do not strike at the little lifts unless this is all you are getting. Wait and see if any of them will develop into a full lift. Small fish could be to blame, and too many false strikes could spook your quarry.

It may be that as the season develops and the fish become wary of the margins and anglers you will need to fish at greater range. The methods of presenting baits at varying ranges described in other chapters will serve well. Boiled baits as used for carp are proving very effective if the right one is chosen.

Of all the longer-range methods that have been developed for tenching, swimfeedering has been the most successful.

The Drennan Feederlink, illustrated in Figure 74, was designed specifically for maggots and is one of the most effective. Figure 75 shows how to modify it for use with any particle bait. With one of these three designs of feeder you should be able to present any bait you choose. The rig illustrated in Figure 92 is very simple and can be adjusted to suit the varied conditions you may meet – such as weed, silt and clear gravel bottoms. Hook-tail lengths can be adjusted from short, say 6 inches, for preoccupied early-season feeding,

to 36 inches or more for shy-biting mid-season tench.

A reliable form of bite indication is essential to ensure that you have a reasonable chance of connecting with any bites you may get. Swingtipping is one way and is illustrated in Figure 35. Alternatively, a light bobbin-type indicator as shown in Figure 34 combined with an Optonic indicator offers a very sensitive bite-detection system. After casting, ensure that your line from rod tip to bait is sunk – prior soaking in a solution of washing-up liquid helps – and clip on the indicator, setting it so that it is approximately 18 inches or so below the butt ring, engage the bail arm, set the clutch and engage the anti-reverse.

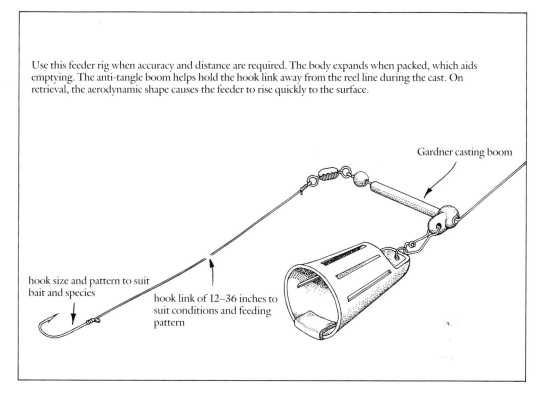

Use this feeder rig when accuracy and distance are required. The body expands when packed, which aids emptying. The anti-tangle boom helps hold the hook link away from the reel line during the cast. On retrieval, the aerodynamic shape causes the feeder to rise quickly to the surface.

Gardner casting boom

hook size and pattern to suit bait and species

hook link of 12–36 inches to suit conditions and feeding pattern

Fig 92   Daiwa Harrier open end feeder rig.

Mike Woods with a male tench of 4lb-plus, taken on bread flake on the lift method.

A 5lb-plus tench taken after dark on a small boiled bait link-legered on the edge of a gravel bar.

Adrian Morley slips back a brace of tench into their beautiful estate lake home.

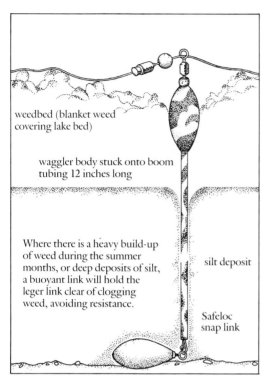

weedbed (blanket weed covering lake bed)

waggler body stuck onto boom tubing 12 inches long

Where there is a heavy build-up of weed during the summer months, or deep deposits of silt, a buoyant link will hold the leger link clear of clogging weed, avoiding resistance.

silt deposit

Safeloc snap link

Fig 93   Buoyant leger link.

Sit down beside the rod or rods and be ready to strike the moment the bobbin begins to move.

The Optonic is not compulsory, but do use a rod rest of the type illustrated in Figure 32. This will allow free passage of line, ensuring you get good bite indication without spooking the fish.

If you have chosen the most appropriate swim, bait and method you should be able to catch tench without too much difficulty.

If you have any reasons to doubt the effectiveness of the rig in use, try one of the others illustrated throughout the rest of this book, but give each a fair trial before chopping and changing.

Bite indication may vary from water to water and according to the time of season, from positive slow unfaltering lifts of the float or indicator to fidgety twitches. Trial and error will be the only way to decide how to come to terms with the latter in the particular conditions, so do not be scared to experiment.

10 Night Fishing

There are various reasons for night fishing. The two most obvious are the availability of time during the week and the location of the fishery. Many anglers fish from the early evening into the night, possibly up to midnight or just after, because they cannot fish during the day-time and must go to work the following morning. Many anglers who do not have a good local water to fish during the week travel to their chosen venue on a Friday evening to fish through Friday night till some time Sunday. To maximise their chances they fish through both Friday and Saturday nights.

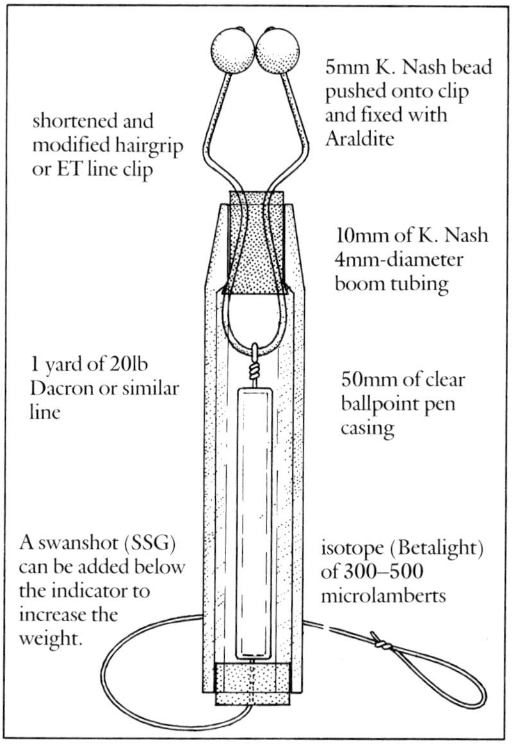

There is another reason for night fishing but this is one which possibly very few night-fishing anglers have recognised as yet. What most anglers come to observe during their longer fishing sessions is that more fish seem to fall to their baits during the periods of darkness. Depending on the type of water, there may be a logical reason for this. It may be that daytime activity drives the fish out of range of the baits on day-ticket waters. If limited night-fishing access is allowed to a small group of anglers, the fish may feel safe moving back into closer range to feed on all the free bait, which provides easier fishing. It is very rare to find a water where *all* the fish are caught after dark.

Anglers who catch most of their fish after dark should observe whether other anglers are having the same results. If others are catching during the day it may indicate a shortcoming in the bait or terminal tackle of the angler who catches only at night. It may be that the rig is too obvious; it may not be presenting the bait as it should; perhaps it is the wrong rig for the swim; maybe the bait colour is too bright and obvious, particularly if it is one that has been well used and successful to the point where the fish spook simply at the sight of it. If you go night fishing simply because you are unsuccessful in the daytime, take a long look at your terminal tackle and bait

Fig 94 Leger indicator with isotope (Betalight) for night fishing.

Labels in figure:
- shortened and modified hairgrip or ET line clip
- 5mm K. Nash bead pushed onto clip and fixed with Araldite
- 10mm of K. Nash 4mm-diameter boom tubing
- 1 yard of 20lb Dacron or similar line
- 50mm of clear ballpoint pen casing
- A swanshot (SSG) can be added below the indicator to increase the weight.
- isotope (Betalight) of 300–500 microlamberts

colour and try changing some aspects of the presentation. Observe the general appearance of the lake bed where it is visible. Clear water means that your presentation must be natural whereas coloured water, like darkness, takes the edge off the fishes' visual senses, which lets you get away with poor presentation. If you have any doubt have a chat with the other anglers on your water. If approached sensibly, an angler who is catching might well point you in the right direction. Take care not to make a nuisance of yourself, though.

The most obvious aspect of night fishing is that in the dark you cannot see what you are doing or where you are casting. To get your bearings, you must prepare for a night session during the daytime or the early evening. The amount of preparation depends on how long you intend to stay at the waterside. In this instance we will limit our preparation to cover a single overnight session. Once you have had some experience of that you can decide whether or not you would like to fish longer and prepare yourself accordingly.

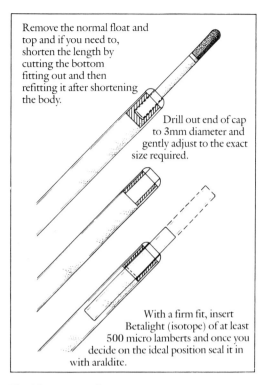

Remove the normal float and top and if you need to, shorten the length by cutting the bottom fitting out and then refitting it after shortening the body.

Drill out end of cap to 3mm diameter and gently adjust to the exact size required.

With a firm fit, insert Betalight (isotope) of at least 500 micro lamberts and once you decide on the ideal position seal it in with araldite.

Fig 95   Isotope float.

TACKLE AND SUNDRIES

Most tackle is the same as for daytime fishing. Sundry items such as spare terminal tackles, baiting needles and baits must be easy to find in the dark, and one of the best ways is to lay them all out on a white cloth or plastic sheet to one side of your fishing position. To help see what you are doing you should equip yourself with a small pocket torch or one of the clip-on flexible torches. Never use a large torch or Tilley-type lamp, too much light will disturb other anglers and create a blindness beyond the light of the lamp. Small spots of light allow your eyes to readjust to the dark more quickly after use. Bite indicators will need some illumination. On bright moonlit nights simple white indicators will be reason-

ably visible but on dark nights you will benefit from fitting isotopes (betalights) of a power of between 300 and 500 micro-lamberts. These can be fitted into special sections of many of the purpose-made monkey climbers and night floats available in most tackle shops. Terminal tackles can remain the same, and so can lines – though it may pay to increase the main line by a couple of pounds BS to protect against snag damage.

PREPARATION

Once you arrive and choose a swim it is a good idea to make some exploratory casts without a hook to discover any possible snags, and then make a mental note of their position. The next task is to line up the point in the swim where you will position your baits and make a note of the background so that you can line up with background silhouettes after dark. Tackle up and make a cast to the exact point you wish to fish. Then make some mark on the line to indicate the exact distance for when you have to recast after dark (particularly important if you are casting to a bar, an island or the far bank margins).

There are several ways of doing this – nail varnish applied to the line, or an elastic band or strip of electrical tape wrapped round the line on the spool to trap it (useful in daylight, too). With the nail varnish you can feel the line as it slips through your fingers. Check the

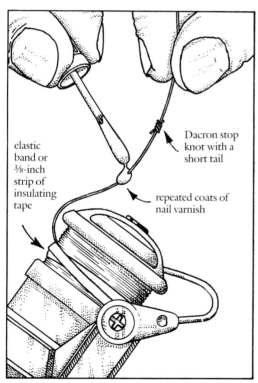

elastic
band or
⅜-inch
strip of
insulating
tape

Dacron stop
knot with a
short tail

repeated coats of
nail varnish

Fig 96 Marking distance on line for night fishing and accurate casting.

line travel by pinching down to stop it and reel back any line to reposition the bait on the correct spot. A Dacron stop knot with a short tail can be used in the same way. With the elastic band or tape the cast will end with a slight jerk as the line comes up against the band or tape. With practice, the strength of the cast can be controlled to minimise the jerk, allowing smooth presentation. If correctly set, with a few loops of line on the top, you can then set your indicators to whichever method you are using. If you use tape, use a narrow strip about ⅜ inch wide and set it towards the back edge to allow line to be taken if necessary by a running fish.

With these key points organised, bait the swims you are going to fish and place your hookbaits in position, then place yourself in the best position to deal with a run if it should come. Arrange your seating close to your rods. A folding bed-chair is useful but can encourage you to relax too much, with the risk of falling asleep. Bivvies are another item to be used for longer sessions only. They encourage you to be too far away from the rods and if you doze off in the warmth you may not get to the rod quick enough to stop a fish reaching a snag and you may end up injuring or losing the only fish of the session. The best way to fish is to sit beside the rods, prepared for the slightest activity. It can be tough, but if you cannot stay awake or alert you should not be night-fishing.

Your landing net should be either placed ready in the margin or stood in an easily accessible position. Lay out your unhooking pad in a suitable place and possibly lay out your weigh-sling, scales and perhaps a keepnet or carp sack. All this will save a lot of hunting around in the dark.

When casting into tight areas where accuracy is paramount, make the final cast just before dark to ensure that a fresh bait is in position. Once it is in place, leave it there until a take comes. The less casting, the fewer mistakes and tangles. If you have a take and need to recast, the markers will help get it as near perfect as possible. A distinct advantage can be gained by using bait stringers at night to ensure that your hookbait is near some free offerings. Tie some ready for use and store them separately.

Take plenty of warm clothing, food and drink. It is surprising how cold it can get on a clear August night!

THE ACTION

When a take comes deal with the strike in the normal way. Once in contact with the fish, get close to the water and get down low so that you can see the rod silhouetted against the skyline. In this way you tell which way the fish is moving. Conduct the fight carefully and remember the position of any snags, bars or obstacles. Once the fish is close in, lay the net out and gently coax the fish right over it before lifting. Don't use any light at this stage – it could spook the fish and cause you to lose it. Once the fish is netted, release the bail arm, lay the rod in the rests, carry the fish to the unhooking pad and unhook it quickly. If you wish to weigh the fish do so quickly and, depending on its size, either release it or retain it in a suitable keepnet or carp sack, remembering to ensure that it is upright and comfortable. Check any of the retained fish regularly until you are ready to photograph it.

If you have followed all the advice you should get some good photographs before returning your fish safely. You may well be encouraged to give night fishing some extra effort in the future. But, remember, be sure that you are fishing at night for the right reasons – you will probably enjoy your daytime fishing all the more.

11 Handling and Fish Care

With the current cost of good-quality fish of all species running at an alarmingly high level, it seems very surprising that more is not published on the subject of handling and fish care. Most articles or books on coarse fishing seem to miss this point or if it is discussed the subject gets the briefest mention in the midst of the recollection of memorable captures. Perhaps writers should be criticised but when you are trying to put over all the other points that make stillwater fishing what it is it is very easy to overlook the subject.

To be fair, there has been a debate in the monthly magazines on the subject of injury and possible death of big carp caused by dangerous types of fixed-lead bolt rigs. With these rigs, if a reel line breaks above the fixed leger weight – perhaps it parts during the cast or is snagged by a hooked fish – your quarry may be left trailing the bomb, which can become immovably snagged, tethering the fish until it either tears the hook free with severe damage to itself or ultimately dies from exhaustion and starvation.

In the excitement of hooking, playing, landing and handling what might be the biggest fish in the water we are all prone to lapses in concentration. Big or small, *all* fish deserve the same respectful treatment. Every fish we catch should be carefully landed, unhooked and returned undamaged. They are scarcely to blame for their predicament: you placed the bait and hook out there in their environment.

You never know exactly what you have hooked until you get it into the landing net. Many of us have thought we were playing just another small fish, only to discover that it is a carp of over twenty pounds. So respect each fish you hook; you might just get a surprise the next time.

Fish care begins with the method employed to hook them. There is always a chance that something may go wrong. Ensure that rods and lines are balanced and that your line is in good condition. When tying up rigs, make sure that the knots are as strong as possible.

The rigs to avoid are those which cannot be shed if the line breaks. The use of silicon rubber to hold the bomb onto the swivel ensures that if a breakage occurs and the bomb becomes snagged the fish can pull free and only trail a length of line, which will hopefully be removed at the next capture.

Balanced tackle, with the rod's test curve matched to line of the correct breaking strain, helps to eliminate a lot of the risk of breakage and the loss of baited rigs. Using tackle suited to the range you intend fishing at also helps prevent problems. At close range a softer-actioned rod will prevent breakage should a strong fish bolt during the fight. Check regularly that the clutch is operating freely. Many anglers overlook or forget the fact that temperatures – hot or cold – can affect the performance of the drag systems on most reels. You may set the drag just tight enough in the cool of the early morning only to find

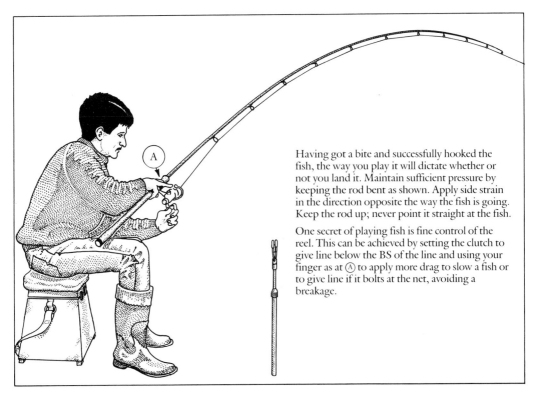

Having got a bite and successfully hooked the fish, the way you play it will dictate whether or not you land it. Maintain sufficient pressure by keeping the rod bent as shown. Apply side strain in the direction opposite the way the fish is going. Keep the rod up; never point it straight at the fish.

One secret of playing fish is fine control of the reel. This can be achieved by setting the clutch to give line below the BS of the line and using your finger as at Ⓐ to apply more drag to slow a fish or to give line if it bolts at the net, avoiding a breakage.

Fig 97   Playing a hooked fish.

that it does not give line in the heat of the midday sun, risking a breakage if a fish should bolt.

Finally, ensure the tackle you use is strong enough to allow you to prevent fish getting into snags, lilies, tree roots, and so on, and to allow you to play the fish quickly to the net. There is no credit playing a fish for thirty minutes or an hour; all you are doing is expending the fish's energy and causing stress and a build-up of lactic acid, which may cause severe distress and possible death from exhaustion. Be equipped to play the fish hard for the shortest period but take care to play the fish with caution at close range. Excessive force at the wrong moment may break your line or, worse, rip the hook out, tearing the

fish's mouth. You may witness fish with split mouths during your fishing. They look horrible to us. Just consider how the victims must feel and take care accordingly.

LANDING

Once you have played the fish to the margins and are about to net your prize it is essential to use a net of sufficient size and suitable material. It may seem obvious that a good-quality landing net is important, but some anglers go ill equipped. The wrong handle or the wrong mesh can equally contribute to the injury or loss of fish. Too short a handle may mean that you are unable to reach over weed or down steep banks. An extending telescopic handle may seem over-fussy to some anglers, but it can pay to carry one of at least three sections extending to a total of about 10 feet. You may not need to use the whole length, but do not get caught short!

Landing nets need a little thought. A fairly open, micromesh pan net is superb, and the bigger diameter the better. Diameters of 18 or 20 inches are ideal for all species, though a triangular net with 36-inch arms may be necessary for carp. The round-shaped net gives you an equal chance of getting the fish in from any angle; a triangular net has limited angles of access. Never lift a fish on the line over marginal snags, except for small roach. You risk losing your fish and perhaps injuring it.

HANDLING MATS

Once you have netted your catch, unhook it swiftly in the landing net supported on your knees and either return it or retain it. If it is a good fish take it to a soft grassy area for unhooking. If necessary, lay out a handling pad like the one marketed by E. T. Tackle, which will ensure that the fish is not damaged by gravel, twigs, or the like. Use a good pair of forceps or a disgorger to release the hook.

PHOTOGRAPHING

After the capture of any fish, particularly a quality fish or a quality bag, you will have to

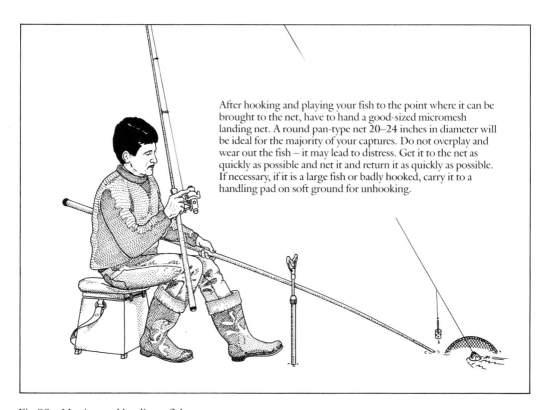

After hooking and playing your fish to the point where it can be brought to the net, have to hand a good-sized micromesh landing net. A round pan-type net 20–24 inches in diameter will be ideal for the majority of your captures. Do not overplay and wear out the fish – it may lead to distress. Get it to the net as quickly as possible and net it and return it as quickly as possible. If necessary, if it is a large fish or badly hooked, carry it to a handling pad on soft ground for unhooking.

Fig 98   Netting and landing a fish.

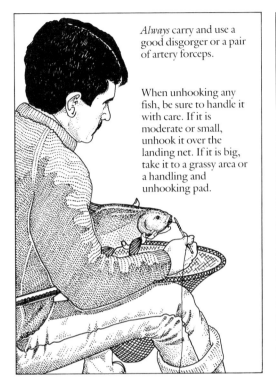

Always carry and use a good disgorger or a pair of artery forceps.

When unhooking any fish, be sure to handle it with care. If it is moderate or small, unhook it over the landing net. If it is big, take it to a grassy area or a handling and unhooking pad.

Fig 99   Unhooking over a landing net.

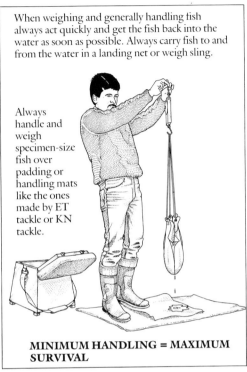

When weighing and generally handling fish always act quickly and get the fish back into the water as soon as possible. Always carry fish to and from the water in a landing net or weigh sling.

Always handle and weigh specimen-size fish over padding or handling mats like the ones made by ET tackle or KN tackle.

MINIMUM HANDLING = MAXIMUM SURVIVAL

Fig 100   Weighing and handling.

decide whether to simply weigh, photograph and return your fish or retain it for a while.

KEEPNETS

If you decide to retain your prize you must keep it in a way that will not injure it or cause it any distress. The smaller species, roach and rudd, will not come to any harm in a keepnet, provided it is large enough – at least 18 inches in diameter and 12 feet long and of micro-mesh material. At a pinch tench and bream can cope with a short period in a keepnet. If you intend using a keepnet, make sure you use one of the type described and stake it out with a rod rest so that the fish can move around freely.

KEEPTUBES

The bigger carp, tench and bream may suffer discomfort if kept in a keepnet. If you really must retain them, one of the larger carp sacks or one of the new pike or barbel tubes (tubes of the carp-sack nylon material covering a set of hoops similar to a keepnet) is to be preferred. They offer the fish the comfort of a keepnet without the risk of their fins being split or their flanks roughened from rubbing up against the mesh. The dark material excludes a lot of the light, which keeps the fish passive. The nylon material is full of punched holes, which allow the water to flow freely through the tube. Probably the biggest advantage is noticed when you come to release your fish: you simply untie the end

119

The season about to close and Graham Dumble and Glen Barnard contemplate what their catch might weigh in a year's time.

opposite the one you put the fish in. It saves the effort and the discomfort of getting the fish out backwards. As with keepnets, the tube should be positioned in deep enough water and staked out with a pair of rod rests.

NEED TO RETAIN FISH

The main reasons for retaining your fish are likely to be to accumulate a large catch of rudd or roach, perhaps, or one or two large specimens of a particular species for a photograph. Whilst this is natural, consider whether it is to the advantage of the fish,

particularly with big fish in shallow water during the summer. If in any doubt, return your capture quickly. Photographs are the main goal when big fish are retained and some thought about how to go about it can prevent both disappointment for the angler and discomfort for the fish.

PLANNING YOUR PHOTOGRAPH

Careful planning of where the shot will be taken – a pleasant backdrop of reeds, a bush or some other bankside feature – will enhance the shot. Make sure that there is plenty of soft grass or matting to lay the fish down on. While you are looking and planning, make sure that your catch is comfortable in the water. If you are planning to photograph the fish as you catch them and then return them it may be necessary only to leave them in your landing net while you or a friend set up your camera. Whichever choice you make, have everything ready and in position *before* you take the fish out of the water.

With all the camera equipment ready, remove the fish from the sack and swiftly get a secure hold on the fish to prevent it wriggling and thrashing off the mat. A good move is to cover the fish's head with the sack to quieten it. Once it is quiet, pick the fish up, placing one of your hands round the wrist of the tail and the other round the snout, with your palm underneath. A big carp can be calmed if you place your index or middle finger in its mouth. The fish tends to suck at the finger, which allows you to lift it slowly. If you feel that the fish is going to wriggle and thrash, put it down on the mat and quickly cover it with the carp sack until it quietens down, then continue as before. You should be kneeling on the mat and should only lift the fish to just above your knees, about level with your waist. Take your photographs quickly; do not pose and play around with the fish. Get some good photos on the bank and then slip the fish back into the sack and take it down to a suitable piece of bank or margin, perhaps taking a final shot of the release. Some really good photographs can be taken at the water-side, and shots of the release of your prize are particularly rewarding. Please do not spend time messing around on the bank setting up cameras with the fish out of the water. You don't want trophy shots of dead fish.

RETURNING FISH

When you release your fish spend enough time supporting the fish to make sure that it is fully recovered and able to swim. A tired, exhausted fish just shoved back into the lake could be in desperate trouble.

A THOUGHT FOR THE FUTURE

If you go prepared with good equipment and terminal tackle to hook and land your fish, and then handle and return them with respect, there is no reason why you or any-body else for that matter should not catch them again, as many anglers before you may have done.

We all love to catch fish that have never been caught before and, whilst there is always the chance of finding a few, you must take care of them.

Because of the number of anglers fishing today many of the fish we catch are caught regularly. Many of them were caught for the first time by anglers seeking uncaught fish. Clearly they returned them unharmed. It would be nice to think that we will all do the same.

Appendix 1
Baits, Ingredients and Recipes

High-protein and high-nutritional-value (HNV) ingredients

Lactic casein (various grades available)
Sodium caseinate
Calcium caseinate (Casilan)
Lactalbumin
Egg albumen
Soya isolate
Soya flour
Wheat gluten
Equivite (milk pellets)

Pruteen
PYM (Philips yeast mixture)
Brewers yeast (Healthilife, etc.)
Shrimp meal
White fish meal
Meat and bone meal
Molasses meal
Peanut meal
Robin red
Trout pellets

Particle and mass baits

Hemp
Tares
Black-eye beans
Maple peas
Chick peas
Peanuts
Tiger nuts

Cashew nuts
Haricot beans
Butter beans
Sunflower seeds
Dun peas
Buckwheat
Pumpkin seeds

Soak *all* the above for twenty-four hours and cook *all* the above until soft enough for hooking – test bait during cooking to assess condition and note the time for future reference.

Add flavourings and sweeteners, etc., to the water when soaking and cook in the same water.

High-protein bait recipes

7oz Casein
1oz Equivite
1oz Egg albumen
1oz Calcium caseinate

5oz Casein
2oz Equivite (pellet)
1oz Lactalbumin
1oz Soya flour
1oz Calcium caseinate

APPENDIX 1   BAITS, INGREDIENTS AND RECIPES

Mix with six eggs (max), adding colouring, 5 millilitre of flavouring and 5 millilitre of sweetener to the egg before the dry ingredients. Introduce dry ingredients slowly to the eggs, mixing and adding in stages. Allow mix to stand 5–10 minutes. Roll into balls and boil for ½–2 minutes. Use within twenty-four hours or freeze and use within twenty-four hours of defrosting.

Flavourings

Regular flavours

Almond	Fenugreek	Maple cream	Sweetcorn
Aniseed	Golden syrup	Milk	Treacle
Butter	Hazelnut	Peach	Tuttifrutti
Banana	Honey	Peanut	Turkish delight
Cream	Liver	Pineapple	Toffee
Cinnamon	Malt	Strawberry	Tiger nut
Caramel	Maple	Sea fish	Walnut

Ethyl alcohol flavours

Juicy fruit	Fresh shrimp	Cornish ice-cream
Strawberry jam	Sickly butter	Sweet plum
Fresh pineapple	Salmon	Cherry top
Black cherry	Red rum	Bun spice zest

Use of flavours should be kept to the minimum, taking note of the concentration levels from individual suppliers – 5–10ml maximum to a 1lb mix. Higher levels could become repellent. Add sweeteners to suitable flavours in dose of 5–10ml to 1lb of bait.

Pet-food-based special baits

8oz Munchies	6oz Trout pellets	4oz Sluis universal
1oz Sodium caseinate	2oz Sodium caseinate	4oz Sluis mynah food
1oz Gluten	1oz Soya flour	1oz Sodium caseinate
	1oz Gluten	1oz Gluten

Mix the above with 4–6 eggs, adding colourings, flavourings and sweeteners if you feel the need. Alternatively, leave the bait in its natural form and allow the base flavour to leech out. Roll the mix into baits of the size you require and boil for ½–2 minutes to obtain the hardness you require.

Floating baits

Pedigree Chum Mixer	Kelloggs 'Start' cereal
Pedigree Chum Small Bite Mixer	Kelloggs 'Golden Nuggets'
Felix Crunch	Munchies
Purina 'Sea Nips'	Go-cat

With the biscuit-type pet foods there is a difficulty in attaching them to the hook. This can be overcome by soaking them prior to use. To do this place the amount you intend using into a plastic food box, perhaps 4oz, and cover briefly with boiling water. Pour the water off and seal the box. Shake the contents vigorously for a few minutes to prevent them sticking together. If you wish to boost the attraction or change the flavour, add a couple of millilitres of flavouring and sweetener to the container during the shaking. In a couple of hours the bait will be soft enough for easy hooking.

APPENDIX 1 BAITS, INGREDIENTS AND RECIPES

Floating special bait mixes

4oz Munchies
3oz Sodium caseinate
1oz Gluten
½ tsp Baking powder

2oz Caseine
3oz Soya flour
2oz Sodium caseinate
1oz Gluten
1oz Equivite (pellets)
½ tsp Baking powder

With both mixes 6–8 eggs will be required. As an alternative to making a full batch, place 4 eggs in a mixing bowl, add any flavourings and sweeteners required at this time and whisk together. If colouring is required add this to the dry mix. Slowly add the dry mixed ingredients to the eggs until a consistency of thick soup is achieved. Pour this into a greased baking tray and place in a preheated oven set at 190°C for a period of 20–30 minutes until risen and sufficiently cooked. Remove and allow to cool.

GROUNDBAIT

Brand Name/Use and Characteristics

Red Angler's Crumb Like all this range, it mixes to provide plenty of bulk and is perfect for deep or fast water. The red is rich and designed to work in clear water or in conjunction with casters and red maggots.

White Angler's Crumb Mixes to a perfect white to bring the best results possible when mixed with any of the Masterclass additive range. A versatile groundbait for all waters.

ADDITIVES

Brand Name/Use and Characteristics

Bream Feed Turns a rich red colour when mixed. A very versatile additive suitable for all waters and types of coarse fish.

Katch A great favourite that has been improved even more. Rich in ground hempseed, it is a terrific additive for roach, carp and tench. Mixes to a very dark shade.

Meatymix Designed especially for use with meat hookbaits. It is rich in protein and has a strong luncheon-meat flavour. Fantastic for carp and tench.

Feedabait Specially formulated for use with swimfeeders. It explodes from the feeder as it hits bottom. One kilogram can be blended with up to 1kg of groundbait.

Red Feedabait Similar to normal Feedabait but turns a rich red when mixed. Great for clear water use and in conjunction with casters, worms or red maggots.

Bronze Feedabait The bronze-coloured alternative to the other two Feedabait additives. Try this one with bronze maggots or in coloured water.

Superfeed Ideal for hard-fished waters and a popular choice with match anglers. Its strong mixture of attractors works with most coarse fish.

Bronze Bream Feed A favourite suitable for all coarse fish. Very effective with bronze maggot hookbaits. Mixes to a golden bronze.

Bloodworm Superfeed Mixes to a bloodworm red. Works well with bloodworm hookbaits but just as effective with other baits. A good choice in clear water or on difficult waters.

All the above are available from the British Groundbaits Masterclass range in 1kg packets. They should be used in conjunction with either of the listed groundbaits or any of the other groundbaits in the Masterclass range. If you buy your breadcrumb loose or grind your own, the additives can be blended with these. 1kg of additive can be mixed with a maximum of 2kg of groundbait.

Appendix 2
Useful Addresses

National Association of Specialist Anglers (NASA)

Membership Secretary: Kathy Fickling
Kilgarth
27 Lodge Lane
Upton
Gainsborough
Lincolnshire

National Record Fish Committee (NASA)

Chairman: Phil Smith
155 Hunts Lane
Coventry
Warwickshire
Tel: 0203 687780

Pike Anglers' Club of Great Britain (PAC)

Secretary: Neville Fickling
Kilgarth
27 Lodge Lane
Upton
Gainsborough
Lincolnshire

British (Rod-Caught) Record Fish Committee (NAC)

Peter Tombleson
11 Cowgate
Peterborough
PE1 1LZ
Tel: 0733 54084 (Day)
0733 252428 (Evening)

Anglers' Cooperative Association

President: Allan Edwards
Midland Bank Chambers
Westgate
Grantham
Lincolnshire
NG31 6LE

RECOMMENDED BAIT SUPPLIERS

Nutrabaits
95 Main Street
North Anston
Sheffield S31 7BE
— oils and base mixes available from tackle shops and direct

Geoff Kemp Bait Ingredients
Pilgrims Court
Days Lane
Pilgrims Hatch
Brentwood, Essex
Tel: 0277 74291
— ingredients, flavours and base mixes available from tackle shops and direct

Tony Osborne
Particle Baits
1 Morley Road
Sutton
Surrey SM3 9LN
Tel: 081 644 7747
— beans, nuts and seeds, etc. available direct only

Further Reading

Arbery, Len, *Catching Big Tench* (David & Charles).

Bailey, John, *Roach – The Gentle Giant* (Crowood).

Bailey, John, and Miller, Roger, *Bream – Tales and Tactics* (Crowood).

Bailey, John, and Miller, Roger, *Perch – Contemporary Days and Ways* (Crowood).

Batten, David, *An Introduction to Carp Fishing* (Crowood).

Batten, David, *An Introduction to Pike Fishing* (Crowood).

Batten, David, *An Introduction to River Fishing* (Crowood).

Cacutt, Len, *British Freshwater Fishes* (Croom Helm).

Coster, David, *Anglers' Mail Guide to Coarse Fishing* (Hamlyn).

Fitter, R., and Manuel, R., *Guide to Freshwater Life* (Collins).

Gibbinson, Jim, *Modern Specimen Hunting* (Beekay).

Head, Len, *Tench* (Crowood).

Maskel, Peter, *The Best of Dick Walker's Coarse Fishing* (David & Charles).

Paisley, Tim, *Carp Fishing* (Crowood).

Plummer, David, *Tales of a Coarse Fisher* (Oxford Illustrated Press).

Pullen, Graeme, *Guide to Freshwater Fishing Baits* (Oxford Illustrated Press).

Walker, Richard, *Stillwater Angling* (Pan).

Wheeler, Alwyne, *Freshwater Fishes of Britain and Europe* (Kingfisher).

Whieldon, Tony, *Coarse Fishing* (Ward Lock).

Wilson, John, *Go Fishing* (Boxtree).

PROTECT WILDLIFE • TAKE LINE HOME

Index

Italic numerals denote page numbers of illustrations

INDEX